I Don't Know . . .

I Was Just a Kid

BY

Thomas J. Gilday

I Don't Know . . . I Was Just a Kid

Edited By
William J. Napier

*Thanks Bill, without your
technical assistance and endless patience,
I could not have completed this project.*

International Standard Book Number: 1-932864-03-2

Library of Congress Number: 2004110255

Published by
Masthof Press
*219 Mill Road
Morgantown, PA 19543-9516*

DEDICATION

It makes me sad
that my mom won't get to read this.

August 6th, 2003
at 9:25 A.M.
Mom-Mom went home.
Everyone loved her,
And had good reason.

If love is the currency of life,
She is a very wealthy lady,
Who earned much,
Spent lavishly,
And left a fine inheritance to all who knew her.

FOREWORD

"Children Are"

Many an hour has passed me by,
In but the twinkling of an eye,
It was long ago, but I recall,
Those precious years when I was small.

The countless nights before I slept,
As through the darkness starlight crept,
And my mind would stray so far,
Guided by each shining star.

On a motionless fancy's flight,
Drifting through the soundless night,
All the world I'd see and greet,
Parading there beyond my feet.

Seeing each new sight and wonder,
Sharp and clear as claps of thunder,
Dancing bright before my eyes,
In their many shapes and guise.

So green a land, so pure and fair,
Blemished not with adult care,
A land without restraint or bind,
Nestled within each child's mind.

So much I envy their recluse,
And how I wish my soul were loose,
How many times in vain I pray,
To be but blessed as free as they.

Oh what love and kind compassion,
Had the Lord that He did fashion,
Every child in every nation,
With his own imagination.

T.J.G.

Chapter One

I was born and raised in Philadelphia. Let me say, W.C. Fields not withstanding, it was, in those days, a wonderful place to be a child.

In this day and age of neighborly indifference when anyone can live anywhere, it doesn't matter, because wherever you live, you're all alone. The last street I lived on before moving out of the city, there were between forty and fifty families living there. I knew two of them and a couple more who I could smile and nod to before turning and hurrying on my way without a kind word between us.

The city has become a scrambled mass, a totally unconnected mob of individuals living together, yet all alone. This is sad, but true. You can live in a neighborhood or even on a particular street for years, and never know the people that live down the block. You know what kind of car they drive, or if they have a dog that barks. But that's about it. This condition, unfortunately, even includes the kids. Children may play organized sports in a group, or belong to Scouts, or a church youth group, but it's not the same as it was when I was growing up. As often as not, the members of these organizations do not live close enough to one another to play together on an "unofficial" basis. I say all of this to point out how different life in the *"City of Brotherly Love"* was when I was growing up. But then again, I was just a kid, so what did I know?

The city's make-up was different. There were rows upon rows of middle-class homes, some upper middle-class, some lower middle-class, but all working-class families. Families who raised their kids, kept their homes, paid their taxes, played by the rules, and supported the system. Those taxes and that support not only made the neighborhood, but the whole city, a thriving and promising place. It promised a good life, and most often, it delivered.

The "rock" that all of this was built on was those families, those neighborhoods, and those people. Different races, different nationalities, yet they were all the same—they were families. We had all manner and sort of families. We had white ones, black ones, yellow ones, and a large number of in-between-shades from dark brown to light tan. The thing that united us was that we were all families. We had a kind of common understanding because we had the same problems and the same aspirations. For any and all of our differences, we were the same. We were all family. We were all Americans.

Chapter Two

My family lived in a small row house on a small street in a small neighborhood. The neighborhood was small, not because of the physical size, but because of the attitude of the people. Almost everyone knew everyone else . . . at least, well enough to know what street you lived on, what school you attended, or where your father worked.

Speaking of my father, he was a short man, but thickset and strong. He had black, curly hair, a kind Irish face, and a loud, infectious laugh that boomed through the house. It made you join in the laughter even when you didn't know what was funny; a wonderful gift and a joy to all. I have a nephew who along with a tremendous sense of humor, inherited my Dad's joyous laughter. It warms your heart when you hear it. There's nothing as funny as listening to him watch a comedy. I immediately think of my Dad. I have many loving, kind, and funny memories, and a few heartaches, but all in all, I chose well when I picked my Dad.

Everyone has a favorite memory, and I, too, have one. In those days, there were many unique ways to make a living. One man's answer was a merry-go-round on the back of a truck. For a

Bologna Row

penny or a nickel (today it would be a dollar), you could ride while a record player provided a lively tune. It operated, not by a power take-off, or by a little motor, but by old-fashioned arm power. A big round hand-crank powered the ride, and if you were nice, he would let you turn the crank. Wow! What a thrill! One of my dearest memories as a child is of the guy we called the "HURTY GURTY MAN" and his wonderful machine.

It was a warm summer afternoon and almost time for dinner. I was standing watching that merry-go-round go around when I became aware of my Dad standing there watching me. Funds were usually tight, so impulsive spending was never the order of the day. He smiled and asked if I had my eye on a particular horse. I did; the black one with the white mane. He fished around in his pocket, paid my fare, picked me up, and put me on the ride. It was an unplanned kindness . . . a little extra for no reason . . . no big deal, but it sure was to me! I often wondered if he even remembered it, or if he had any idea how much it meant to me. It makes me wonder how often we do things that we don't think about or remember—things that have an impact on others, for good or ill, for the rest of their life. A little scary isn't it? It makes me want to pay more attention to what I do and say. But, then again, what did I know? I was just a kid.

Chapter Three

M y father worked at Philco, Plant C, making radios, and then later televisions. He worked there and so did lots of other people in the neighborhood, including my Mom. In the beginning of the industrial spread of the city, large areas of the city were like small company towns with nearly everyone working in the same factory. People had to live close to where they worked. Public transportation was so poor and private transportation, if it existed at all, was even worse. So, out of necessity, people would tend to cluster near where they worked.

Within these work areas, the local neighborhoods sprung up. The neighbors were mostly friends and relatives, people with similar backgrounds, people who attended the same church and belonged to the same political party. In other words, people just like me. I don't remember anyone being excluded as much as being included. As a house on the block was going to become available, someone told cousin so-and-so, and so on it went. All the other neighborhoods were the same. In a neighborhood near where I lived, an area maybe six blocks square, there were three Catholic churches, and three totally separate neighborhoods—one

Polish, one Irish, and one Italian neighborhood. Three separate cultures . . . three separate languages. They went to separate grade schools taught by nuns from three separate countries. Yet, as they grew up, they belonged to the same boys and girls clubs, went to the same high schools, and later worked at the same jobs, and at night, they each went home to their own neighborhoods . . . neighborhoods filled with people just like them. I won't discuss the rightness or wrongness of this social order. That is a valid subject for discussion, but one for a smarter head than mine. In those days, in those neighborhoods, it was a good way to grow up.

I roamed not only the neighborhood, but the whole city fearlessly, because for the most part we had nothing to fear. All of those houses were full of families just like mine. I sometimes played with kids in other neighborhoods, so I knew. They spoke different, and sometimes they looked different . . . but still they were just like me. The big ones were moms and dads—just like mine—and the little ones were kids—just like me. Wherever I went and whomever I met, I felt no reason to fear; after all they were just people like me. The world was a warm and familiar place, and I was comfortable in it . . . but then, what did I know? I was just a kid.

Chapter Four

The street where I lived was a little street. The cross streets at both ends kept it from being a long street. One block long, little more than an alley wide—but that one block was the whole world to a little kid. There was an official name on the street sign at the end of the block, but to us, it was just Bologna Row. We knew everybody, and everybody knew us. All the people watched out for each other, and everyone watched out for the kids. The houses were small, and made of brick with marble front steps. It was just four rooms with an outhouse. The sidewalks were brick, the street was Belgium blocks, and street lamps were gas (later converted to electric). It's amazing that such a small, humble place could hold such joy and so many memories.

It seems as if it should have been larger, a little grandiose or something. I went back to look at it recently, it was even smaller and less impressive than I remembered. Although at the time, to us it was very grand. The rooms were square and seemed "spacious." I guess because they held all we had and all we needed. This we considered "plenty." Although some may have called us poor, we never knew it. We thought we were well off and often prayed for the poor children. There I was, in hand-me-down clothes, with a shine on the seat, and a hole in the pocket, taking pennies to school to help feed the "starving Armenians." I'm glad we were just kids and didn't know any better. Growing up is the time to learn, and we learned lots. We learned to make do with what we had, and to appreciate what we had. We learned to enjoy and most importantly to share what we had. For a bunch of poor kids, apparently, we had a lot and learned even more.

Chapter *Five*

Once one of my uncles came into possession of a large number of woolen pullover sweaters, his pay, no doubt, for a week's work at some sweat shop or on a hot loading platform. People were often paid in strange ways, but were glad to get it. These sweaters were red, white, and blue, with an Indian chief on the front, and an Indian in a canoe on the back. They were various sizes so that no matter what your age or size, there was always one appropriate to be handed down or passed around.

We wore those darned things everywhere . . . all the time. In the fall of each year, we all walked around smelling like mothballs. When they were new, they went to church and school. As they began to fade, we wore them to play. When we went anywhere in a group, we looked like a team.

After a few years, and countless washings, they became not only ubiquitous, but unique in color. As they faded, they turned sort of maroon, pink, and purple. We used to joke about the sweaters that reproduced in the bottoms of closets and that there were so many, we would never outgrow them. In our old age, they would haunt us. We thought we would still be wearing them in the old folks' home. What I wouldn't give for just one of those old faded Indian sweaters with the smell of mothballs and all.

This was not an isolated incident. Whenever someone came into an abundance of anything, it was shared up and down the street. Now it's easy to look back and say that with only an ice box or tiny refrigerator, you couldn't store things anyway . . . you might as well share them. This may be true, but I chose to believe that they would have done so anyway. There was closeness, a concerned caring about one another. If there was a sickness or a death in the family, the neighbors knew and did what they could to help. Whether it was babysitting, a pot of soup, or sudden good fortune, we shared and felt better because of it. Often one or other of the men on the street would get a day's work somewhere and be paid in fruit, vegetables, or some other goods. This was shared with all the neighbors, whether it was a bushel of peaches, a crate of cherries, or an endless supply of Indian head sweaters . . . we seemed to understand that "plenty" was more if you shared it.

Chapter Six

The diminutive (I got tired of saying small) kitchen was situated in such a way that the morning sun shone through the window curtain and turned the whole room a hazy shade of yellow. On the windowsill, the ever-present pan of rising dough and on the stove, its mate, the coffee pot.

From the basement, there was the faint odor of a coal fire and from the floor the smell of Fel's Naphtha soap and Pine jelly. When I think of this scene and remember those wonderful smells, I think of Saturday mornings. My Mom, Dad, and I, along with my red Radio Flyer wagon, would go to the local American Store to get the week's groceries. After we returned, there would be coffee and three different kinds of doughnuts from one of those grocery store boxes. The coffee was freshly ground, and packaged in a paper bag with a folding top.

I remember the first time my Dad gave me coffee instead of milk with my doughnut. He made a great production out of getting out a cup, pouring the coffee, the milk, and sugar. There are chefs on T.V. now who don't make as big a deal out of making a full-course dinner. With great flourish, he presented me with my first grown-up cup of coffee. It was very sweet with more milk than coffee—but it tasted just great! If I try really hard, I can still taste it. I was a big guy now . . . all mature and grown up . . . but what did I know? I was just a kid.

Saturday mornings were magic. They were magic days in a magic kitchen full of lights and shadows, warm familiar smells, meals with long conversations, tall stories, short jokes, and endless laughs. When I think of my family together, above all other things, we laughed. It's still that way today, as I pray it will always be. A little laugh goes a long way and does its own magic . . . whether or not you are just a kid.

Chapter Seven

While I'm on the subject of magic, we had a magic lantern in our little house. Our magic lantern sat at the bottom of the stairs that led up to the bedrooms. It had a glowing amber light and in the dark could take you anywhere in the world. It could, and often did, take us to strange and wonderful places.

Like most homes at that time, our radio was the source of real magic. At night, when I was supposed to be in bed, I would lay at the top of the stairs, looking at that glowing light and listening to the magic. Cops and robbers . . . cowboys and Indians . . . Amos and Andy, and Fibber Magee and Molly. (They now sell these old-time radio shows on tape.) I can't begin to tell you the number of whole shows that I remember. I guess it shouldn't be surprising when I think of all the time I spent lying on the floor with a make-believe cigarette (a piece of wicker broken off from a clothes hamper) blowing smoke rings and dreaming dreams. In those dreams I was in Duffy's Tavern or on Wistful Vista, or sitting in the back of Jack Benny's Maxwell. Awake I listened, asleep I dreamed, wonderful stories replaying in my head. It's amazing how very clearly these scenes played in my mind. For the amount of good those nocturnal adventures did for the imagination, I would not hesitate to recommend late night radio as a school subject.

The long hours of cool darkness, the smooth feel of a well-scrubbed wooden floor, and the soft flicker of the amber dial light were both comforting and nurturing to mind, body, and soul. I believe it was at least as good for me as the sleep I missed.

Somehow, as if by magic, I would always wake up, in the morning, in my own bed. It was just recently that I realized my Dad must have put me to bed every night and never said a word. You see, he loved the magic lantern too.

Chapter Eight

I was just a kid, but I remember blackout curtains, curtain stretchers, linoleum on the floor, and the smoke of wood fires in the air. While I think about the air, I remember when horses delivered milk, bread, butter, and eggs; and hucksters sold fruits and vegetables and all manner of things. I remember the ice man who brought the wherewithal to keep all these things fresh.

The leftover residue, along with all other refuse, including the ashes from the furnace, were hauled away by wagons pulled by great sweating horses . . . horses that left an air of their own. Crossing the street was, at times, an adventure. I've often thought this contributed to my learning how to dance. I remember dance contests at block parties, and winning dishes at carnivals.

In those days, some dishes came from strange places . . . gas stations, boxes of detergent, and from the movie theater when it was "dish night." Sometimes, if the movie was appropriate, and most of them were, one of us kids would get to go with my parents. For ten cents admission, we saw a double-feature, a serial, a newsreel, a travelogue, or other special feature, a couple of cartoons, previews of coming attractions, and during the war, the bond drive.

Sometimes they would even interrupt the show to play Amos and Andy on the radio. All of this and a dish too! Not too bad for a kid with a dime! The movies were great entertainment whether I went at night with my parents, or Saturday afternoon with my sister, Rita. The entire experience was an adventure in imagination, from planning to recovery. The one exception was "The Saturday Chore."

Before we could go to the movies or any other fun place, we had a job that had to be done. The entire universe would have fallen out of balance if we failed to scrub the front steps. The front steps were white marble and easily got dirty. Apparently, in that strange day and age, the entire world judged the worth and character of your family by the amount of sparkle on your front step. There were a considerable number of agents involved in the process. There was a scrub brush, bleach, cleanser, the ever-present Fel's Naphtha soap . . . and last, but not least, a bucket of water. All up and down both sides of our little world, kids were up to their armpits in scouring powder and suds, making all well with the world.

When at last we were finished and had the "mother's seal of approval," we were free to start thinking of a movie selection, movie money, and movie permission. We usually took the secret shortcut to the movies, and it only took twice as long and guaranteed that you would arrive dirty and a little scraped up.

Well anyway, it got you in the proper mood to see a movie classic—something involving horses and heroes no doubt. There was no shortage of Republic Pictures stars; Bob Steele, Lash LaRue, Wild Bill Elliotte, Johnny MacBrown and JOHN WAYNE. All the way home we were the characters from the movie. Sometimes we were Zorro and the bad guy, or Fred and Ginger, or Roy and Gabby. Whoever we were, the spell lasted until we got home for dinner. Sometimes, we just made it in time to get ready to eat dinner. If we took the shortcut home, it took a little longer, but we didn't dare come home late. The family sat at the table together. Nothing else was even considered; it was dinner time.

Chapter Nine

Dinner was a big milestone in the day. The family always sat at the table, cleaned and pressed and each in their places. Sometimes dinner was prompt and moved right along, and sometimes it was slow and lasted a long time. Never was it so hurried that it didn't include conversations. Dinner was a break in the day and an opportunity to get together and "catch up" on each other. After dinner, the pace of the day changed. There were different games for before and after dinner. Before we ate, we usually got our bath and clean clothes. Then afterward, we played calm and "clean" games like Red Rover, Statues, Wall ball, or some sit-down guessing game. Home base was always the running board of the car parked on the block.

There weren't a lot of cars around in those years during and just after the War. Not many people could have afforded to drive one anyway, because both gas and tires were expensive and rationed. Still we managed to get around somehow without them. The few we did have made great home bases for our street games. During the day, the before-dinner games, all stops were out. We could play Follow the leader, Buck-Buck, or go on a bike hike.

I must confess that calling our little expeditions a hike would be like saying Lewis & Clark took a little walk. We would pack a lunch, a bicycle and tire repair kit, and set out by dawn's early light. We usually ended up in a creek skinny-dipping or somewhere on the far side of wherever, then arrived home late, tired, and starving. Sometimes we went exploring on foot, no place we should have been, that's for sure.

One of our wilderness trails was "The Old One Trackey." It was a long abandoned railroad spur which went nowhere, but it sure was fun going. Running along either side was a drainage ditch, full of tadpoles and countless other neat things. Guaranteed, the trip would get you dirty and skin the knees out of your dungarees.

Some games were "crossovers" and so they were fair game to play anytime. At times they just spontaneously erupted and spread like an epidemic. Games like "Freedom Tag." This game had different names in different neighborhoods, but the game was the same. It involved a base or prison into which prisoners, that had been tagged, were put. If you could touch base and shout "freedom" all the prisoners were free. If the person or team who was "it" tagged you in the process, you went to prison.

Somewhere along the way, children have lost the ability and the desire to organize street games. Growing up in the city, street games were an elaborate rite of passage. There were complicated rules that varied only slightly from one neighborhood to another.

At times in the summer, there were twenty or more kids involved in a game of Freedom Tag. There were surprisingly few major disputes. I say major disputes because there was always

"I tagged you," "No you didn't, you missed me," etc. . . . etc. . . . etc. There were many, many games and few fights. It didn't take much to amuse us . . . a half of a pimple ball and mop handle and a Half ball game would start.

There were any number of ball games; Wall ball, Hand ball, Box ball, Football (with a rolled up newspaper), and Tire ball (played not with a tire but with a small piece of garden hose). The girls played Hop Scotch, countless games of Jump Rope, and endless games with a ball. Speaking of which, there's one thing I'd like to know that I haven't yet been able to find out. Who *is* O'Leary? What does he have to do with the Postmaster? And how did they get involved with bouncing a ball? All of my growing-up years, I've heard girls sing a song while bouncing a ball: "One, two, three, O'Leary . . . Four, five, six, O'Leary . . . Seven, eight, nine, O'Leary . . . Ten, O'Leary, Postmaster."

With very little raw material and no outside prompting, games would just seem to happen. As more kids came along, they grew or changed into games more suited to the number. Again they would change as the younger kids had to go home to bed. Sometimes the games would last for several days. Marathon games of tag often ended after dark and started again the next day after supper. We were well organized for a bunch of kids who didn't know much. We knew what fun was and we knew how to have it. No electronics, no coaches, no expensive programs, no adults at all, just a bunch of kids having a bunch of fun . . . but then again, what did we know?

Chapter Ten

While I'm on the subject of spontaneous fits of organization, let me point out that they were not all restricted to games. There was the summer of the TITANIC. Oh it didn't start out that way, but "the best laid plans of mice and man. . . ." That whole summer was spent building, from scratch, THE U.S.S. INVINCIBLE. Never have you seen such an assorted mountain of supplies. There were Tinker Toys, erector sets, model kits, Popsicle sticks, and a bunch of leftover pieces of balsa wood, and more, lots more. Some of it was useless and most of it questionable, to say the least. The one thing you could not question was the enthusiasm.

All through the long hot summer, with a number of fits and starts, we worked, engineered, experimented, and built. Cellophane from cigarette packs for the portholes, tar from a roofer's kettle for caulk, model car paint, and motors from erector sets. Borrow, "mix match and make do," always the project went forward. This one went to camp, and that one went on a family vacation. Kids came, and kids went, but always the project moved forward. Its home was an empty refrigerator box on a vacant lot. I don't believe there was a single day that summer that there wasn't at least a small gang of workers. Sometimes to redo what had been done the day before, and hopefully, redone correctly this time. Eventually the big day came, the ship was ready, and so were we.

I don't know how many kids there were, but we had a small army. There were kids of every size and description: kids on foot, kids on bikes, kids on skates and scooters, and a small herd of kids on "Push Os" all beaming with pride.

There she was—trim and sea worthy as any Liberty Ship built at the Navy Yard. It was painted red and white with gold lettering. Her proud captain, a lead soldier from W.W.I., was standing tall behind a Tinker Toy ship's wheel. We thought of everything. Now was the time to put up or shut up—time to launch! Off we headed to the riverfront, our proud creation in tow. Some of the bigger kids on bikes went over to the New Jersey side to retrieve our triumphant prize after her first crossing. The rest of us stayed on the Pennsylvania side to attend to the launch. She was christened with the spray of a shaken-up Coke. There were a number of unsuccessful attempts at a speech, shouted down by cries to "get on with it." We placed the noble ship into the water, and with a mighty roar started her engines, and pointed her to New Jersey. Off she went on her maiden voyage, five yards, ten yards, then before our eyes the Invincible turned into the Titanic. The further out she went, the lower she rode in the water. What we had thought of as a cruise ship, a luxury liner, turned out to be a submarine. We could do nothing but sadly watch her sink.

The summer was over and it was time to start thinking of school. Someone in the gang suggested we could build a rocket ship to Mars, but that would be for another summer. Years later, we learned our mistake; when you build a ship you have to soak it in water to swell the seams closed to make it watertight.

Oh well! What did we know? We were just a bunch of kids.

Chapter Eleven

I often do more than one thing at a time. Somehow this helps me to concentrate. Sometimes in church, during the sermon, I make notes to myself. (Honestly, I am paying attention.) I write notes about things that are on my mind. I began thinking about when I was growing up. Later, when I got home, I kept on writing, and thinking, and writing some more. I didn't start out to tell a lot of stories, but it's funny when you get started, stories just come rolling back to you like waves on a beach.

I'm not always aware of them, but there they are just waiting to flood like Noah's rainstorm, a deluge of memories. I was five or six chapters deep before I began to think about writing a book. I have been facing my own mortality recently, and thought I would like to share these memories with you. The nicest thing about memories is that you can share them with other people. Sharing memories is like sharing part of your life, and that makes your life that much more enjoyable. So sit back, get me another glass of wine, the teapot is full, there's coffee on the stove, and get comfortable—I have a few more stories to tell you—stories of the kids from "Bologna Row." (pronounced buh-lōw-nē)

I have no idea where the name "Bologna Row" came from. It was sometimes used as a put-down, but we never thought of it that way. We were proud to be the kids from Bologna Row. I've heard stories about the origin of the name, but I have no idea of their truthfulness.

The story goes . . . during the height of the "Great Depression," one among the many who was out of work and behind in his bills, was threatened with being dispossessed. When the "rent man" came to put them out, he had a couple of workmen with him. They began to carry the furniture out the front door and onto the sidewalk. While they were busy, the men from the block were carrying things around the back and inside again. If they watched the back, things went in the front. If they watched the pile, things came from other houses. After a little while the house had more furniture in it then it did to start with. There was no point in calling a cop, the same thing was going on all over the city. The rent man eventually gave up and left; there was no one to rent it to anyway. The man whose home was the object of this exercise, was forever grateful. Later he was fortunate enough to get a good job in a meat processing plant. He kept everyone on the block well-fed with bologna. We had it fried for breakfast, raw for lunch, and roasted for dinner. Boring, but gratefully filling during a time when having anything at all to eat was welcomed. Bologna Row was a good place to be and we were all glad to be a part of it.

Now, as I said, I don't know how true this is, but it's a great story and . . . I didn't know any better, I was just a kid.

Chapter Twelve

If I'm going to keep on with these stories, I really should introduce the rest of my family. Besides my Mom and Dad, I have six sisters—two older and four younger. Like all kids, we had our little scraps, but all and all I loved them dearly, and still do. If they weren't my family, I would want them to be my friends. They are, from big sister to baby sister: Cass, Floss, Rita, Judy, Miriam, and Donna. Each a special joy in their own way and each a touchstone of memories. To this very day, when we get together we always end up sitting around the table telling stories and laughing. My Mom usually sits with her mouth and eyes wide open saying "that never really happened, where was I when this was going on?" The rest of us enjoy shocking her with our stories and like all fondly remembered tales of long ago, they are all entirely true stories . . . mostly anyhow. After all, we're Irish and can't allow dull facts to interfere with a good story. I know it's politically incorrect to stereotype . . . but I will anyway—the Irish love words. We love poems, songs and stories. We love sad stories and funny songs, or funny stories and sad songs, and poems of any kind. The Irish love words and I guess I come by it honestly. I've been accused of not

being able to say yes or no in twenty-five words or less. I hope not
to be too long-winded but unabashed. On I go with another story.

What a kid!

Chapter Thirteen

The Good Lord watches
over drunks and little children.

As a young boy, I, and my friends, would often go to the waterfront and explore piers, warehouses, abandoned buildings, and empty railroad boxcars. Not recommended playgrounds for children, but we truly didn't know any better. One day, while exploring a boxcar, a friend and I found a large snake in a pile of straw. It was a very, very large snake, maybe an Anaconda. The boxcar had been used to transport bananas. There is a tool used by the railroad brakemen that looks like a baseball bat but with the end flattened. Armed with this deadly weapon, and with the advantage of cool weather to slow him down, we struck down the giant beast. Thus began the "Great Bananaconda Adventure."

Problem: What does a nine-year-old boy do with a large, dead snake? What does he do with a snake that is much larger and heavier than he, and looks, 'for all the world,' like a dragon? Answer: Find a very sturdy cardboard box and tote it home. Well, drag more than carry. The darned thing weighed a ton. It took the better part of the day to get it home, but I persevered. My friend had long since given up and gone on ahead. On and on I struggled. I would have my trophy. I had slain the dragon and I would have his hide. Like all tasks, no matter how difficult, I eventually made it home, my awesome and gruesome cargo in tow.

And now back to the problem: What to do with the stupid thing? The answer came when my cousin and I put our heads together. (My cousin was my dearest friend and almost constant companion while growing up, and a better and more faithful friend a kid never had.) Every Batman needs a Robin, and every Laurel a Hardy. We were at least this for each other and often times more. But whenever there was mischief afoot, we were the first of the "usual suspects" to be rounded up—usually for good reason. We were at the epicenter of more than our share of mischief.

Back once again to the problem. Answer: At the end of the street, there was a vacant lot with trees and weeds and a diagonal dirt path. This path, of course, everyone used to come and go. Aha! An idea! We took the snake out of its paper sarcophagus and laid it on the path with a discarded wire coat hanger propping up its head and holding open its mouth. There sat the monster, ready to strike.

Next, we moved to an alley close enough to see and hear the fun, and far enough to avoid the blame. The first victim approached. It couldn't have been better if we'd planned it ourselves. Our victim was an older (older to us anyway) woman who enjoyed yelling at the kids on the street when play got too loud. She carried tales, and in general enjoyed making our young lives miserable, and thus, she was often the butt of our pranks. It was a mutual antagonism that secretly both sides enjoyed. And now, here she came, heedless

of our ambush, a bag of groceries in one arm, like Little Red Riding
Hood into the woods. Quiet . . . quiet. It took forever for her to get
across that lot. Stop. Look. And Scream! That woman made an
amazing noise. It was painful to the ear and caused dogs to howl.
The bag of groceries went in one direction, and she in the other,
with her skirts hiked up, and beating feet. And oh boy, could she
run! Like a startled deer, she vanished over the horizon, leaving
only that awful noise echoing in our ears.

When we recovered from the shock and the paralyzing peals
of laughter, we knew we had to recover our intimidating property.
As soon as we were able, and with the cardboard box in tow, we
ran to collect the Great Bananaconda.

When we got there . . . it was gone! Frantically, we looked
everywhere. We could find nothing. Time was running out. If we
were going to maintain deniability, we had to scram. Scared spitless,
and in between fits of laughter, we made for a safe spot to think
this thing out. Hard as it was for us to believe, the great snake had
not been dead at all, but only stunned. And now it was on the loose
in the neighborhood hurt, angry and probably looking for some kid
to eat.

Something else that was hard to believe was just how upset
and angry everyone was. It seemed like we were the only ones who
got the joke. There was no way we were about to admit our part in
the current emergency. At first, people were dubious about the story
of a great snake, but sightings came in here and there and soon
everywhere. It became obvious. We had been invaded by a
monster. What followed looked like a mob scene from the movie

Frankenstein. In today's litigious society, someone would call the police and someone else would call his lawyer. In those days it was different. A posse was formed. The older boys, armed with "22 Cal." rifles, BB guns, slingshots, and a motley assortment of long sticks and short ropes, the fearless hunters set off—off to hunt the "snark," or the snake, whatever. We were the only two people in the whole world that knew what had really happened, and all we could do was steal sideways glances and try hard not to laugh. The great snake finally met its postponed fate with much fanfare and boisterous bravado. The poor half-dead beast succumbed. I'm sure it was glad to be rid of nasty little kids, screaming ladies, and fearless teenage hunters. At last, on to its eternal rest, only to be resurrected at family gatherings for lo these more than fifty years. Not too bad for a slithering stow-away from South America. But then, what did it know? It was just a snake.

Chapter Fourteen

Life is nothing if not changing. Our time in the tiny house, where we were born and raised, with all its memories, joys and sorrows, came to an end. There came a day we no longer lived on Bologna Row. I went back to play for awhile but somehow it's not the same. A poet once said, "You can never go home again," you can, but sometimes when you get there, it's someplace else. As small as our old house was, our new house was that big. The basement was as long as the house, which was very long and high enough for a kid to jump and not hit the ceiling. All of this, and it was a half story above ground. Above the basement were three stories, three very tall stories, of very tall rooms that were big in all directions. You could see that house forever, and from the roof, you could see twice as far. My parents and sisters had bedrooms on the second floor, along with two full bathrooms. My bedroom was on the third floor along with several storage rooms. We had more room for storage on that third floor than we had in the old house top to bottom. And so began our adventures in the big house on Lehigh Avenue. No, I'm not going to make the obvious reference to the "Big House!"

We'll go back to the "Little House on Bologna Row" in our memories, the only way you can, but first, let me tell you a couple of stories about life in a different place. Same people, different house. We were just a pack of kids that were glad for the extra room. Life goes on.

Chapter Fifteen

I told you the basement was large and long. There was a long staircase at one end that led to the kitchen, and a short one in front that led to a door to the outside. I was, at that time, a very good shot with a bow and arrow. I got lots of practice. With a large cardboard box filled with old newspapers as a backstop, I set up a target range in the basement. For a long time, it worked very well. What I didn't consider was that if you put enough holes in a box, sooner or later, it stops functioning as a backstop. The front door of the basement was half wood and half glass. The last arrow went through the box, without slowing down, and on through the glass part of the door. As my usual luck would have it, my father was coming home from work. The arrow knocked the newspaper from his hand and continued onto the sidewalk. Needless to say, he was not amused. The target range and the bow and arrow went out of business, and so did I, for awhile anyhow.

One more thing about that basement before I move along— I learned one of the basic truths of life in that basement. As I said, there were two staircases, one led down from the kitchen and the other led to the outside, however, there was only one light switch.

It was just inside the door from the kitchen. One of my jobs, at that time, was to tend the furnace. The furnace in the old house was small and inefficient. This furnace was huge and burned coke. With the size of the house, we needed a lot of heat, and this furnace supplied it. When I was going out, I would leave the light off, go down the basement, tend the furnace and go out the front door. One day while following my little routine, I shook down the fire and put some fresh coal in the furnace and shoveled out the ashes. Then, as I was getting ready to leave, I noticed something glowing bright white. I picked it up to get a little better view. The basic truth I learned was, "Don't pick up anything that glows in the dark unless you know what it is." This glowing object was the metal saw blade from a box of wax paper. When you pick up something that hot, it takes a minute for your brain to get hold of the idea, then, if it's really hot, you have a hard time getting the message through to your fingers, "LET GO." I could do nothing but stand there and cry and make some kind of incoherent noise. The whole experience probably didn't take more than a few seconds but it seemed like hours. It hurt for days. The scar was permanent and so was the lesson.

Although it was hard work, I always enjoyed tending the furnace. There is some kind of primitive satisfaction in taking care of a fire. Our ancestors sat around a fire to tell stories, so I guess it's in the blood. We now sit around the table, although a campfire would be nice, but the stories are still the same. Put another log on the fire and listen to this one.

While I'm talking about fires . . . on the street behind the big house was a vacant lot. Sometimes in the early evening, on a summer's day, all the kids in the neighborhood would gather and build a large bonfire. Now, aside from a beacon to attract all the kids in the area, we used those fires for two main reasons. First, was to bake potatoes that we lathered in mud and buried in the hot ashes. I can honestly say that nothing you have ever had in your whole life tasted that good. Secondly, the fires were used to melt wax. We got the wax from a church in the neighborhood. They would put it out in the trash, and we would rummage through and reclaim it. We made many ingenious things with this wax, but our favorite was molds of our hands. This was accomplished by dipping our hands into the melted wax. For some reason, we thought this was just great. After all the industrious uses were exhausted, the fire was a nice place to sit and talk, or to just sit and stare into the glowing coals and dream.

Chapter Sixteen

Kids enjoy torturing one another. In turns, we each picked on the next younger ones. None more so than Rita and I picked on poor Judy. She was just young enough to be the perfect foil for all of our tricks. If we were upstairs jumping on the beds like trampolines, my father would yell up the stairs, and yell up the stairs, and finally come up the stairs. Being older, we would hear him coming and feign innocence. Youthful enthusiasm being all-consuming, Judy would still be merrily enjoying the delights of the jump when the major eruption went off. She was just old enough to get all the blame.

We all, in turn, did the dishes. When the lot fell to Rita and me, we would talk Judy into doing the dishes for us. The bait was a set of electric trains that were set up in one of the rooms on the third floor. Faithfully and solemnly, we promised that in exchange for her labor, we would let her run the trains. After she had eagerly done her duty, Rita and I would run ahead up the stairs and close the door. "Gee these trains are sure a lot of fun!" In the meantime, poor Judy stood outside in the hallway crying, "You promised!" The next day, was the same thing. We would convince her that we wouldn't have the nerve to do that again. Same story, same result. I don't know how many times we pulled this prank, but Judy swears we scarred her for life. Fortunately, we all survived somewhat sane—even Judy. She grew up to be a fine person and a world-class mom. Her three sons are among the true joys of this life. Their company is always enjoyable, and they're not just kids anymore. They are three very nice young men.

Chapter Seventeen

All of our "hijinx" weren't directed at one another.
We picked on the general public with equal relish.

One year for Christmas I got a fishing rod. Now, on a city sidewalk there isn't much to fish for, but we managed to find something. With the proper alignment of lead weights, and a small, very sharp hook, from the very high third-floor window, Rita and I went fishing for hats. Ladies' big fancy hats were the best but, in a pinch, men's Stetsons worked almost as well. There seems to be a little lag time between when something unexpected happens, while the brain processes what's happening, and before you react at all. This lag time was just enough to reel in the ill gotten goods out of the victim's line of sight. When their hats came off, they looked all around, forward and back, even under parked cars, but no one ever looked up. Eventually, they gave up and started on their way, scratching their heads as they went. That was our cue. We would then sail their hats back at them and duck back in the window in fits of laughter . . . time to get ready for the next fish. Looking back, with what is hopefully a little more maturity, I thank God in His mercy that we never caught an eyeball instead of a hat. Eventually we outgrew it, or went on to some other form of entertainment. It makes me nervous every time I see a kid with a fishing rod. I pray he isn't as dumb as I was. "Dumb" and "Lucky" . . . I think they'll probably be my lawyers when I face St. Peter at the Gate. I hope they can talk fast, Heaven knows, I'll need it.

Just a dumb kid fishing for answers . . .

Chapter Eighteen

My Mom was a wonderful cook. Now I know everybody's mom is a wonderful cook, but natural prejudices not withstanding, my Mom could do more with less than any living soul. We never had much in the way of money, but we always ate like royalty. She made soups and stews and outrageous casseroles—an endless store of secret recipes. Like magic, she could take a steak that would be served to one person in a fancy restaurant, and feed the whole family, and we each had plenty. The bane of my Mom's existence was to go to the grocery store and spend "X" amount of money, but not have whole meals. To still have to go to the butcher shop, or wherever, to have all she needed for dinner was more than she could understand. She always felt that after all she had spent she should be able to spread her hands over the bags and make it enough to feed her family. I've heard people argue that the Bible story of the loaves and fishes was just a fable, not believing that so many people could eat on so little food. Let me tell you, truthfully, if my Mom had been catering for Jesus, they would have had gravy on their fish, two vegetables and butter on their bread. My Mom worked miracles with our food on a regular basis. Then again, what did we know . . . we were just a gaggle of hungry kids.

PRAYER

I stopped awhile and knelt to pray,
Then wondered as I went my way,
How many prayers of different kinds,
To think of all, would stagger minds.

Some are echoed long and loud,
A song reverberating clear and proud,
Others are whispered soft and low,
Like gentle flakes of falling snow.

The sweetest prayer, I think of all,
Isn't uttered 'neath steeple tall,
Yet finds its way to God above,
A silent symbol of perfect love.

It wears a coat of glitter bright,
And stands erect both day and night,
Arms outstretched and raised to Thee,
This beautiful, shining Christmas Tree.

T.J.G.

Chapter Nineteen

I've said any number of times that funds were tight, but deep in my heart, I find it hard to believe; maybe that's why I keep going back to it. We always had good food, warm clothes and great Christmases. I once asked my Mom if she believed in Santa Claus. She looked me straight in the eye and said, "You know we've never had any money, but somehow we've always had a great Christmas. I don't know about you, but I believe." Never argue with your mom. As far back as I can remember, our stockings were hung by the chimney with care. It was the one time of the year that I didn't mind having knee socks- the longer the better- and sure enough they would be filled with a tangerine, some walnuts, some pennies, and a toy or two. In addition to the filled stockings, we always got one big item and a couple of small ones, a large, decorated tree and a full turkey dinner—so large that a herd of locusts couldn't eat it in one sitting—but we tried awfully hard.

When we would wake up on Christmas morning, we were not allowed downstairs until my parents gave the okay. They wanted to see our faces—that was their Christmas present to themselves. They had been up 'til all hours preparing all of this bounty. We, on the other hand, had a good night's sleep, were wide awake, and raring to go at the crack of dawn. While we waited, we tried for all we were worth to see down the steps and around the corner. It never worked, but boy it was sure a lot of fun trying!

Christmas was all of this and more. It was a time to bundle up against the cold and trundle out to visit friends and family, to see their trees and all their goodies. One of the treats we often got was something called wine and soda. This secret concoction was made with a few spoonfuls of sweet port wine in a large glass of ginger ale. I often think of this wondrous elixir but am afraid to retry it—afraid that a taste would ruin the delicious ghost of Christmas past. It has been so wonderful to remember that I think I'll keep the luscious memories instead of the taste of reality.

Looking back, it seems like every year my sisters would get a set of toy dishes. Not the plastic ones you see today, these were made of china. They were blue and white and had a little scene painted on them. As well as I can remember, there was a willow tree, a bridge and some little people walking around. Another thing that happened every year was the fight over whether or not we children could eat dinner on the toy plates. I don't believe we ever won the argument, but it always seemed worth the try.

Our Christmas tree always had a ton of decorations. Some of them were new, but most of them were very old and very beautiful. We used to play a game that involved picking a ball or decoration and telling what colors it was, and then the others had to try to guess which one it was. It sounds kind of dumb now, but it kept us busy for hours, especially if you include the time we spent clarifying the rules every game. Children always manage to find a game to play. Funny, I can almost smell those trees from so long ago. It smells good, doesn't it?

Christmas, like so many things in my youth, was magic. When we went to bed, the house was normal, very clean and tidy. The house had been worked on for days, however, nothing special. Then the magic came into play. When we came down in the morning, the tree was up and decorated, the presents were under the tree, and the whole house was decorated. When I say the whole house, I mean my mother would hang tinsel from the light switches. Whatever you do, don't stand still for too long, or you'll get decorated. Tinsel today is colored plastic wrap cut into thin strips but in those days, it was silver colored tin or lead foil. One of the jobs, while taking down the tree, was to reclaim and re-package the tinsel for next year. This was necessary because we used tons of tinsel. We also used sawdust dyed green for the village under the tree. Remember that?

Chapter Twenty

While I'm on the subject of pulling plenty out of a hatful of nothing, let me remember vacations. We always managed a week or two in Wildwood, New Jersey. Wildwood could be a book all by itself. We could call it "Adventures With Sand in Your Pants." So, if I can contain myself, I'll just try to give you a taste of the flavors of those days, and maybe one or two little stories.

When we were all very young, we went by train. Can you imagine my Mom, my Dad, five children, and maybe as many as three friends, all in a row, boarding a train with matching luggage? The luggage was brown paper bags from the supermarket and my parents brought all manner and sorts of things including an iron.

You see, Mom was getting her vacation from cooking, sewing and doing the wash with a hand-crank wringer by going to the seashore where she cooked, sewed, did wash by hand and in general, had it more primitive than at home. Everything she did was labor-intensive. Baking and cooking, all from scratch. Laundry involved cooking starch and bluing and boiling water on the stove. Nothing was easy. The girls' dresses, and my Dad's shirts, were always starched and ironed. When I think of all she did, I think of living on borrowed time. She had to be borrowing time from another day to finish her work for this day, every day. So how did she get her vacation? Easy, she packed up a large brood of unruly children, all of her necessities and put them on a train to the seashore and leisurely spent her time doing all of the same things she did at home, plus babysitting, rendering first aid, and various other services. Some fun, huh kid?

We were lucky enough to know a lady who owned some houses at the shore, and she was kind enough to charge very little. She knew we had a gang of kids, were appreciative, and tried always to leave the place cleaner and neater than we found it, a major undertaking with that many kids.

Once again, we ate very well. We had fish fresh from the ocean, fluke as big as doormats, and fresh vegetables from the Jersey farms (eggplants, corn on the cob, Jersey tomatoes and potatoes). We had fresh baked bread from an Italian grocery store. A trip to this emporium was an adventure and a treat to all the senses. The people behind the counter spoke an exotic foreign language, and we loved to mimic their accent. They were always kind and pleasant and went out of their way to make us welcome. Big, smiling, olive-colored faces offering a taste of this or that, with the strong smell of the cheeses hanging overhead, the sawdust on the floor, and most of all those wonderful loaves of bread—hard and crunchy outside, soft and delicious inside. That bread was so good that it required an armed guard to survive until dinner. There sat my father, armed with a rolled-up newspaper, and my Mom guarding him.

The actual journey to the beach was considerably more involved than Stanley's safari in search of Livingston. There was food, towels, playpens, and heaven knows what all to bring along with us. Somehow or other, we managed the long walk to and from the beach. The day at the beach was long, hot and full of countless adventures; who got lost, who was found, who learned to body surf, who found what, who lost what, who built what out of sand, who knocked it down, and **why** they knocked it down. Later we went home for a cold shower to rid us of sand, a family meal, and maybe a night on the boardwalk. Then we would repeat the process the next day.

Chapter Twenty-One

When we were a little older we got a car—a Plymouth coupe. Yes, all of those bodies in a coupe. My Dad always enjoyed watching people watching us. We just opened the doors and out came an almost endless parade of little people each with their own shopping bag. It looked, for all the world, like a clown car at the circus. My Dad would laugh at the unbelieving stares and the open mouths. Come to think of it, I guess we were pretty funny looking. But we were very proud of that little car.

One year, when I was eleven or twelve, we once again went to the shore. This time I brought along a friend. We had all the usual fun and misadventures, but this particular story concerns the trip home. Everyone, and all their possessions, loaded into that tiny car. The back seat had been removed so that behind the front seat was a space that went uninterrupted through to the back of the trunk. We sat on the floor or whatever we could. We sang songs, told jokes, and squabbled over the seating arrangements. The trip took forever. This trip took even longer. Something went wrong with the car. I think it was a flat tire, but I can't for the life of me remember for sure. Whatever it was, my friend and I were deputized to watch the car while everyone else hiked to a restaurant not too far away.

By the time my father returned, my friend and I had struck up some sort of game or other and it had us fully captivated. Now my Dad decided, for whatever reason, to turn the car around, perhaps to get at the bad wheel. We were supposed to watch the back-up, as we were on a hill. Well, whatever the game we had invented was a lot more interesting than a car backing down a hill. "Yeah, come on back, c'mon back, c'mon back," BANG, right into a ditch. So much for fixing things by himself. Now it involved a mechanic and a tow truck and big bucks that we didn't have. My Dad was so mad that years later when talking about it, his face would turn red and sweat would run down his nose. Eventually, it got to be a funny story, but it took time—lots and lots of time. (I'll tell you more about our small, funny car later on . . . but just now, I'm thinking about the seashore.)

Chapter Twenty-Two

The great Seashore Year!!!!!!!!

It was getting to be a drag, every year the same thing—Wildwood with all my baby sisters. My older sisters went to dances on the boardwalk. No, I wasn't quite ready for that yet, but I was old enough to be getting bored. Fate stepped in. I met a friend. His name, I'm ashamed to say, I can't remember after all these years. It was something like Olly Olson or Sven Swenson. It was so Nordic it was almost a parody of itself. His father, who had been a fisherman in Norway or Sweden, had immigrated to Wildwood and became a fisherman. He had a commercial boat at Otton's Canal. He would go to sea for days at a time and catch all sorts of fish. Wow! How cool is that?!!! He had great stories of his adventurous life on the high sea. His mom was a small kind woman who worked hard and made delicious, if somewhat strange, meals. As our friendship continued he taught me lots of new things. Being a little older than I, and much respected, he never seemed to tire of teaching. I learned how to shuck clams and oysters, how to filet flounder, and how to clean and bone large blue fish. I took lessons on fishing, crabbing, and sailing boats of all kinds.

Now, in preparation for this vacation at the shore, I had hounded my dear old Dad. The poor man got no peace. I absolutely had to have a swimsuit with a little swimmer on it and a shirt to match. He was a veteran of several such episodes with my older sisters and knew the only way to get any peace and quiet was to capitulate. So, no matter what it did to the family budget, I would have my status symbol. Mine was a bright, gaudy yellow with an equally obnoxious shirt to match. I tell you all of this because it becomes central later on in this epic.

Among the many and varied things I learned that summer was how to make money.

One of the ways to do this was to clean and bone fish for people coming back from a day of deep-sea fishing. This was good, but the best and the most fun way to earn money, was to dive for coins. There was a large sightseeing boat that docked in the canal, appropriately named the *Sightseer*. Someone on the sightseeing boat would throw a coin in the water. Whoever was closest to where the coin landed in the water would dive and retrieve the coin. The trick was to dive, from the riggings of a fishing boat, close enough to the big boat to be a little scary, yet far enough in front of it to be safe. Later, we split the take. We made lots of money and everything went perfectly, for a little while anyway. Then showbiz got the better of good sense. Slowly, but surely, as the applause and the coins got larger, I got higher in the riggings and closer to the big boat. This caused the applause and the coins to get larger still. So on and on it went, until something had to "give." Let me dispel the mystery, it was me that "gave." While putting on the grand show,

I made a tiny little miscalculation. I cut it just a tiny little bit too close. The dive was dramatic, and well executed, but I brushed up against the big ship just a tiny little bit. The barnacles cut my hip, leg, and bottom, very painful but not very serious. It wasn't until I tried to climb out of the water that I discovered the real extent of the damage. That large ship had performed a first class "pantsing." My beautiful yellow swimsuit, with the little swimmer on it, was gone. A quick and frantic search of the entire area confirmed the worst. My errant swimsuit had gone to sea without me. I, on the other hand, was stuck in the canal without it. All I had was the matching shirt and several long crowded blocks to traverse before I could rectify my embarrassing predicament. You wouldn't think a little fellow like me could run that fast. Now, for my father's continuing part in this little melodrama. . . . He had been a very good sport the first time through and getting me my swimsuit. However, that little swimmer wasn't even up for discussion the second time around. I rather sheepishly spent the rest of the summer in a considerably less expensive model swimsuit. I also found other ways to make money . . . for a little while anyway.

Boy, that was a great summer!!!

Chapter Twenty-Three

One of many things I don't understand is why attitudes are so different now. What made them change? When did we become a society that lost touch with one another? When and why? How did we let our children lose touch with each other and with the "American family?" It makes me sad that we celebrate what makes us different instead of what makes us the same—one family with different members, but each, and all, with the same hopes, the same American dream.

I often mourn the passing of childrens' street games and all that they represent. They served many useful functions. Kids with different backgrounds learned to get along and to work together. Natural leaders emerged. As the group's dynamic changed, different kids took charge. One of the American traits that helped us win World War II was our ability to improvise and to work without leaders. If something happened to the man in charge, someone stepped in and took over. The other side had to wait until headquarters appointed someone to be in charge. This, in part, I believe, started with the street games we played.

If the British Empire won the Battle of Waterloo on the playing fields of Eton, then maybe America won the Battle of the Bulge on the streets and the games that we played there: Giant Steps on Iwo Jima, Simon Says on Omaha Beach, and Freedom Tag in Berlin and Tokyo. Most of the GIs were just kids, but they taught the world how to play fair and still win . . . but it was no game. It's nice to know that some things don't change. G.B.O.T.

Chapter Twenty-Four

Something else I mourn is the loss of Halloween. Yes, I know we still celebrate the holiday, but it's nothing like it was. We didn't get the numbers of treats that kids get today. Candy was a big deal and having bags full of treats was something to dream about in anticipation.

Plans were made days ahead of time. Our memories were thoroughly searched for clues. Who gave generously and who did not? First we hit the houses, then the stores, and finally the bars—giving the patrons time to get a little mellow. All through the long days before, plans were made and revised. Costumes too, had to be planned and created. These were not cheap plastic things now sold in every store, but full-fledged works of art, planned and executed by we, the wee people.

When finally the big day came and the bewitching hour approached, we were ready. A quick dinner, and at the first streak of the shadows of nightfall, we were off like a herd of turtles, like squatters in a land rush, greedy little gremlins on the prowl, in ever enlarging circles with home as the center—we scavenged. People would invite you in and ask you to sing or recite or whatever in exchange for a handful of candy or a big slice of cake, a piece of fruit, some pennies, and treats of all sort and manner. The very idea of someone putting something harmful in a cupcake just never occurred to us. After we hit all the houses and stores, we went to the local bars and other than asking us to sing or dance, no one ever bothered us. In fact, they seemed to enjoy us and were very generous with their change.

We would often travel so far from home, it was necessary to stop at the house for a new bag. We found the energy to perform this feat by eating copious amounts of our swag on the trail, especially things that might not keep in the bottom of the bag with apples dropped on top of them. In this case, there was only one answer: grab that big slice of pie and eat it. It's a wonder that our little stomachs survived, but they did, and not too much the worse for wear. It was surprising the number of people who remembered us from year to year. When I think of how far we went, we never had a thought of harm.

I mourn Halloween and pity our children. They should be able to go anywhere and fear no one. But they can't, and never will. I was able to grow up taking it all for granted. What did we know? We were just a herd of very lucky kids in homemade costumes. "Trick or Treat" . . .

Chapter Twenty-Five

Far from having to fear anyone, I think as an adult I would be a little scared of me as a child. As with most children we managed to get ourselves into occasional hot water. Most of it, we deserved. In fact, I'm sure we deserved more than we got. But, like all super heroes, we also had our nemesis—the same evil lady that scared our poor snake. She spent an inordinate amount of time spying on us from behind the curtains in her front window until she had the goods on us. Then she would wait a little, and stroll casually down the street armed with all the naughty details. "I just thought you would want to know. . . ." My cousin and I were often the object of her hobby. Mostly we earned it, but on some occasions we were innocent.

Enough, after all, is enough. We hatched a plot to discredit her once and for all. Across the street from where she lived was, for a time, an empty house where we sometimes played. Behind this house was an alley, as there was behind our houses. We lived next door to one another and on the same side of the street as our intended victim. Knowing approximately how long it would take for her to get herself together and down the street with her story, we were all set. Mission Impossible, eat your heart out.

We had waited until the time and circumstances were perfect. Our moms were out on the front step talking to each other. We were on the front steps reading comic books and talking. Other children played nearby on the sidewalk. Quietly and without notice, we slipped inside our houses and out the back door. By way of the alleys, we made our way to the empty house. Then in front of the window, we lit cigarettes and blew smoke into the air. When we were sure we had been seen, we ran out the back and via the same alleyways down to the corner and into the back of our houses. Now the *pièce de résistance*. While we were running home, we chewed up a mint candy and spit the juice on our hands and quickly splashed in a puddle to remove the stickiness. We were ready for the final act. Slipping one at a time onto the front step, there we sat as innocently as two newborn babes. Just like we had planned it, everyone thought we had been there all along, and both our breath and hands smelled sweet. Our moms listened with a great deal of patience and then coldly dismissed her, there was no evidence to support her story and we had been sitting there the whole time. The conclusion was that she blamed us for everything and saw us where we clearly had not been. The hardest part had been not to laugh at the critical time. Success! Our evil foe was forever discredited . . . for the time being anyhow.

We went on to many other adventures, most good, some not so good, but always fun, and never too malicious. As for our nemesis, she had to find a better way to spend her time. It wasn't as much fun since her stories were always suspect, but still she couldn't resist the occasional try.

Chapter Twenty-Six

My Mom was a love. Like my sisters, if she wasn't a relative, I would have liked to have her as a friend. She is one of those people that animals and small children just take to naturally. If there is a baby nearby, it's on her shoulder. Imagine a sweet, little old gray-haired lady on a pogo stick. That's right, a pogo stick. One year for Christmas, one of my younger sisters got a pogo stick and my dear, sweet, gray-haired mother took it out on the sidewalk just to try it out . . . it worked.

Among my earliest memories of my Mom is when I was very young, too young to go to school. My sisters would come home for lunch, and after lunch when they would go back to school, my Mom would rest on the sofa and I would rub her back. We would listen to the radio, a cowboy show . . . "Don't Fence Me In." I would rub and sing along with whomever. Rest period never lasted long. There was always too much work to be done. I don't know how women did all they did. Nothing they did was easy. It all required great skill and energy. I remember endless piles of wash while cleaning this and that and all the time a big pot of soup bubbling in the background. Whoever coined the phrase "the good old days" obviously never tried to keep a house in the good old days. As long as I knew my Mom she had a bad back. Although extremely painful, she never let it slow her down. If there was a vacation or even a day trip proposed, she was game and could keep up with the best of us. She is a fun person to travel with and can make the best of any situation. The same sun that melts wax hardens clay. You can choose to complain or to enjoy yourself; it doesn't take a genius. . . . Neat Lady Huh!

Chapter Twenty-Seven

I just now thought of something.
A few stories ago, I mentioned a "Push-O" and I realized
that a lot of people may not know what a "Push-O" is.

A "Push-O" was an ingenious homemade scooter. It was made from a board, maybe three feet long and perhaps two or three inches wide, a wooden box (soda crates worked well), and one street roller skate. Not the new inline skates with urethane wheels, but the old street skates with iron wheels that fit onto your shoe with a skate key. First the skate was taken apart, and then two wheels for the front and two wheels for the rear were attached to the board with nails, the bigger the better. Then the box was fitted on so that the bottom of the box faced forward. Sometimes handles were added to the top end of the box. From this point on, individual creativity took over, usually in the form of soda bottle caps made into elaborate designs like skull and cross bones, initials, or whatever you could dream up. They were often painted, and once again, anything was fair game, like WWII bombers, they some-times had names painted on the front.

One other thing about them; push-o's were loud. A herd of them could be heard long before the scene could be seen and to say nothing of the noise emanating from the big mouths of the little children. Everyone had their own theme song, especially going down a steep hill, and our neighborhood was no exception. Our steep hill was in McPherson Square, a small park surrounding a public library. We called it . . . all together now . . . "DEAD MAN'S HILL." (Spooky music fades in, then dramatically out again.) It was steep enough to scare the "bejeebers" out of you and paved with cement filled with large stones. All the long way down that hill the vibrations were incredible. Even after you reached the bottom, your hands and feet could still feel the shaking and the trembling. Each of us had our own theme song, dramatic music to hum while in danger, like going down a steep hill. In the case of "dead man's hill," between the vibration and the cold fear, the musical composition suffered somewhat. It never slowed us down however, on our homemade ponies. We rode the range in our little neighborhood, with one worn out sneaker.

Chapter Twenty-Eight

In this time of terrorists and tragedies, there is no shortage of spirit, that's for sure. There are plenty of things to worry and upset you, but along with the bad, there comes some good. People display the flag and yellow ribbons. They openly admire and appreciate the military, the police, and firefighters. The general attitude reminds me of WWII. We were patriotic. We loved the flag, home, mother and apple pie, and we didn't care who knew it.

I was very young during the war, but I remember so many things that happened. Most clearly, I remember: blackout curtains, air raid wardens, ration stamps, war bond drives, savings stamps, war maps in the newspapers, stars in the windows, honor rolls, victory gardens, scrap metal collection, saving fat renderings, v-mail letters from overseas, serious talk on the radio, and parades in red, white and blue crepe paper.

One night during the war there must have been a loud noise, because we kids all woke up. All the lights were out and the dark green blackout curtains were pulled down. My parents were nowhere in sight—something we had never seen before. First, we tiptoed all through the house . . . nothing . . . no lights, no radio, no

Mom and Dad. Surely, there were German spies involved, or an invasion, or something equally frightening. There we sat on the floor, in a circle, in the darkness, considering one evil possibility after another, scaring ourselves and each other out of two years' growth.

Fortunately, at this point one or more of our parents appeared. Soon both were calming and comforting their panicked brood. They had just been next door visiting and running back and forth checking on us. No reason for panic, no danger, no spies, no Nazi storm troops. But it was a lot of fun being so scared—for a little while anyhow.

The war for us was a great adventure. It was a time for partings with salty tears, and sweet homecomings with an equal number of tears of joy. It was a time for war stories, Gold Star Mothers, and food ration books. It was also a time for mysterious packages from overseas. One day, in late spring, a package came addressed to me. My Mom and I opened it, eyes wide, our fingers fumbling with crumpled newspaper in a foreign language. It seemed strange, the language was different but the newspaper was the same. It had pictures of the war and maps with big arrows and little flags. Underneath the crumpled paper, there it was. A real German battle flag complete with bullet holes, a fancy dress dagger and a German aviator's helmet. WWII airplanes were not very well insulated against the cold and aviator's helmets were made of leather and lined with lamb's wool. We had a hot summer that year. I had an even hotter one. I must have sweated off ten pounds. My folks did everything short of using a big stick to get me to give up my helmet. No luck, I wore that hat all day, all the time, everywhere. One good thing, I was pretty easy to find on the beach. I don't know whatever became of that hat or the flag, but I still have the fancy dress dagger, it sits on my bookshelf with a lot of other dusty, old stuff. But I remember when it was new.

Chapter Twenty-Nine

Still on the subject of knives, I came across one at a yard sale. It was exactly like the one my Mom had. I remember so well how she had gotten it. There was a popular radio show about a lovable know-it-all. He designed this knife as part of the show. It was a knife, a saw, and a spatula. He then offered it to the audience at the end of the show. Just send in a box top from the sponsor's product and some small amount of money and wait for your treat. The days dragged by while waiting for the package. I raced home from school everyday for two or three weeks. Funny, I don't remember too much about having the darned thing, but I remember the waiting, and I remember the day it arrived. I had learned the joy of anticipation. Truly sometimes the waiting is even better than the having.

Sending in box tops for treasures was a big part of the radio experience. I once sent in for a ring with a telescope on it. Another time, I sent for a ring that decoded secret messages. But the real treasure on the radio *was* the radio and its shows and characters. To sit alone with a radio and listen with eyes closed, you could see all the people and all their props. Sometimes the radio characters would make a movie. This was a difficult thing because in your own head you knew exactly how they looked. What their dogs and houses and everything else about the show looked like. The real actors seldom lived up to your imagination. The picture in your mind was so clear and so vivid that the real actors never could have measured up. TV is great, and I'm glad we have it, but TV is a passive entertainment. You just sit there and it happens. Radio, on the other hand, is active. You have to get involved. If not, it's just noise in the background. You have to actively listen, think about what you're hearing, and then imagine what it would look like. The images were better than real life and have lasted to this day. I knew every one of those characters and to me they were all real. Among my fondest memories are those pictures in my mind's eye: "The Shadow," "Duffy's Tavern," "Fibber McGee's Closet," "The Fat Man," "Straight Arrow," "Jack Benny," "Lights Out," and so many more. Go ahead, add your own favorite. They're all great, I feel so lucky to have been there to hear and to see them all . . . even if I was just a kid.

Chapter Thirty

Philadelphia was a wonderful place to roam . . . and roam we did. With no money in our pockets, we would sneak onto the El (subway elevated trains) and ride downtown. Downtown was a wonderland so big and so different from the neighborhood where we lived. There were rows of department stores. The list of stores seemed endless. They stretched from City Hall to the Delaware River. There were no department stores in the neighborhoods and there were no shopping malls. For minor shopping you went to small local stores. For major purchases you got dressed nicely and went downtown. Those stores downtown had very elaborate displays, regular shows, with puppets, music and the whole works. One store had a massive pipe organ and gave regular concerts, another had an animated village. You could wander from show to show all day long. There were all manner and sort of strange people. It was a day's entertainment just watching them. Another of our favorite diversions was the museums. Philadelphia had a lot of museums, and we sneaked into most of them. We never had a problem doing this, I think more often than not, they turned their backs and winked. After all, who wants to keep a kid out of a museum. To this day I'm a museum freak. In spite of myself, it was a great educational experience. I learned a lot and I learned to appreciate a lot of things by sneaking into museums. I guess it was our version of "surfing the Net." Come to think of it, with the help of "www@Whatever.com" I'm still sneaking into museums. "The more things change" . . .

Chapter Thirty-One

Another favorite spot in the summertime was the Swim-O. Where this custom of adding "O" to things came from, I don't know, but the public swimming pool was called the "Swim-O" and the scooters were "Push-Os." If you had a problem with excessive liquid refreshment, you were a "Wine-O." A young boy was called "Boy-O." To this day my sisters will sometimes call me Boy-O. Maybe it's from the Irish, but everyone in the neighborhood used these expressions.

The Swim-O was a public swimming pool that allowed neighborhood children to swim for two or three hour periods of time. Then everyone had to clear out of the pool to let the next crowd in. The trick was to get out and dry your bathing suit so you could sneak back in. This was how they checked for admittance. If your swimsuit was wet you were not allowed back in. All manner and sort of scheme was tried. Laying them in the street so cars would run over them and wring them out was just one of the schemes. There was a lot of wringing and swinging going on between swim periods, but at least it kept us busy and clean. I don't remember ever seeing a backyard swimming pool; it just wasn't even on the radar scope. We did, however, have large round galvanized tubs, intended for doing wash. These substituted for both a bath tub and a swimming pool, in addition to doing the wash. We got our money's worth out of those old tubs. They hung outside the backdoor of every house on the block, when they weren't full of water and kids. Oh yeah! They made great drums too but, don't get caught banging on them. You could end up with a sore bottom.

Chapter Thirty-Two

Growing up in Philadelphia, I never knew that we had an accent. When I was in the service, as soon as I began to talk someone would pipe up "You're from Philadelphia, aren't you?" "Yeah, but how did you know?" "You all talk alike." I thought people from Brooklyn or the Deep South had a peculiar way of talking, but not me, ya know? I mean, yous guys know what I mean? Yo, we love da Igles, da Flyas, soft pretzels, wooder ice, and cheese steaks. BUT! We don't talk funny . . . ya think? Yez'll be sorry if yous laugh at us.

One more thing that growing up in a house full of kids taught us and that was how to laugh at ourselves. It's hard to take yourself too seriously when someone is standing by, ready to make a joke out of whatever you're stressing over. I think it would be a good thing if we could all chill a bit and laugh at ourselves. If you are able to laugh at it, most things will work out O.K.! Start with a smile, you'll like it.

I think that if I learned anything over the years, I've learned that a good sense of humor covers a multitude of sins. It has helped me get through school as a child, and through life as an adult. Nothing in life helps to build a friendship like sharing a good laugh, not a little chuckle, but a great rollicking belly laugh. Heads of state should start every important meeting with a really big laugh. There would be a lot less trouble in this world if we had a Secretary of Silly instead of a Secretary of Defense . . . or maybe just a funny little kid from Bologna Row.

Chapter Thirty-Three

At one end of our block, like so many other blocks during WWII, was a victory garden. In one corner of the garden was an honor roll. It was a billboard like the ones you see outside of churches that listed the names of all the men in the area who were in the service. Next to their names were different colored stars. The stars denoted who was overseas, who was injured, and who had made the ultimate sacrifice. I remember small groups of us working on the garden. It was neat and tidy and a pleasure to look at and to smell. There was a miniature picket fence painted white like the honor roll. The vegetables grew in well-dressed rows with rich black soil in between them. It was the closest I came to a farm until I retired and we moved to the country. Funny thing, the dirt is still rich and black and it still smells the same. I don't think that we grew all that much in the way of food, but like so many things during the war, it helped us pull together. Gung ho! Whether it was a victory garden or a collection of scrap metal, we all shared the good times and the bad—the dark days of the war and the final victory. There was a feeling that whatever happened, we were all in it together. The G.I., Rosie the Riveter, the man on the street, or a bunch of kids in our victory garden, it was us (U.S.), against the bad guys.

Even if we were just kids, we understood.

Chapter Thirty-Four

At that same end of our block, but across the street from the victory garden, was an American Legion Post. Among other functions, wedding receptions were held here, usually on the weekends. Almost all the men on the block belonged to this Post and with good reason, which I'll get to in a minute. Now you may find this hard to believe, but those wedding parties didn't cost thousands of dollars. They didn't involve caterers or reception coordinators, nor did they include the finest amenities. They were more like families getting together, and for very little cash, pulled off a party. Let's see, there was the hall, a small band usually made up of friends and relatives or a stack of Glenn Miller records, some cold cuts, potato salad etc. (homemade), and of course a homemade wedding cake. For less than one hundred dollars, a lot less, you had a fine time. Oh yes! There might have been a little beer and soda. This brings us to the last expense; a little tip for the men on the block to come in and clean up the place. Early Sunday mornings the gang would gather, brooms, mops, buckets and trash cans at the ready. Everything was wiped and washed from tables to floor. The place was emptied and the trash cans were filled and set out for trash day. Then came the real object of this exercise. The truth be known, never mind the tip . . . they would have done the job for a share of the leftovers. There were always pretzels, chips, food, beer and soda. It gives a whole new meaning to the term "work party," doesn't it?

I loved to go with my Dad to help. One of my jobs was to spread the red oily sawdust on the floor and then sweep it up, with a big push broom. Big brooms, big mops, big buckets and big trash cans . . . everything was big but me. Being small, I was naturally a target for jokes. One of the big jokes was "Tommy would you like a beer?" whereupon they would produce, from behind the bar, a plastic beer. A plastic glass, with a sealed liquid, that looked like a real beer. The men never tired of this prank, and it worked, every time. Because, after the laughter, I got a very large birch beer, on tap, and access to all the pretzels and chips my little person could hold. It was a good deal for both sides. I was paid in full, for all the sweeping, for all the fetching and carrying, and even for the good-natured kidding. After all, I was just a kid. And one thing I did know was that you didn't need a nickel for the juke box, and that it contained a wealth of great tunes. Tunes that echo in the back of my mind and make my heart smile and my soul tap its foot. What I wouldn't give for just one more Sunday morning after church.

Chapter Thirty-Five

Life was not always sunshine and roses. We had our fair share of heartaches and tragedies as well. I remember all too clearly the sad day when my uncle came to our home to tell us that his infant son had died. I don't think I ever knew why he had died. Looking back now and guessing, I would say it was probably S.I.D.S., but I don't know. Whatever the cause, it was sad beyond all belief. It was very disconcerting to us kids, after all, "old people died, or brave soldiers in battle died, but not little children." The funeral was long and tearful. I served as a pallbearer. As upsetting as it was, I was pleased to be a small part of it. I felt that I was doing something to help and that was a good thing.

There was something else that was going on in my young life at that time. I was having a terrible and puzzling conflict. On one hand, I was broken hearted about the baby boy I had played with and visited so often in recent days. It was a bad thing and nothing good could be said about it, nothing good should be said about it. Yet, because of this tragedy, I got my first suit. This was not a "hand me down" not even an "off the rack," this was a tailor-made suit just for me. I even got a hat and trench coat to go with it.

I was so proud of my fine new clothes but I wasn't sure how I should feel. I couldn't talk about it. How could I explain what I didn't understand? All of this I kept inside and did my best to sort out, to accept, and to make peace with. I'm not so sure I ever did. I do know and accept that sometimes there is a sad side to good things and a good side to sad things. Good and evil can sometimes exist in the same event or even the same person, but I still don't know how or why.

Chapter Thirty-Six

I wore those fine new clothes long beyond the time they were fine or new, and long beyond the time they fit. I was especially fond of that hat and trench coat. When I wore them I always felt like "Sam Spade" or "Casey Crime Photographer." I remember once there was a fire in a store around the corner from our house. While everyone ran to the fire, I ran home. Like Superman I had to change my clothes before I could go into action. Never mind the fact that I was wearing dungarees and sneakers, I had my official hat and trench coat. Then to top it all off, I put a piece of paper in the brim of my hat on which I had written, in black crayon, the single word "PRESS." Then with costume on and a notebook and pencil in my hand, I raced to the scene of the big story. Once there, I began to shoulder people out of the way while saying, in my most authoritative voice, "Press, make way for the press." To my amazed delight the crowd parted and I walked to the front, franticly making notes as I went. Even the policeman waved and winked at me, enjoying the show with everyone else. Fortunately, I didn't push the farce any further. With the fire out and the excitement dying, I left the stage still in character. The crowd, to the credit of their kindness, laughed only quietly and left my dignity as intact as my costume. Neat outfit kid!

Chapter Thirty-Seven

Adventures in an Outhouse

Have you ever had the pleasure of attending to your personal business in an outhouse? Let me tell you, you haven't really lived until you've visited the half-moon hotel. They are most often constructed of a single layer of lumber with one or more sheets of tar paper on the roof, and with only the single porcelain convenience. Talk about "no frills," it was basic, uncomfortable, and was guaranteed to be twenty degrees hotter in the summer, and twenty degrees colder in the winter. I've heard it said that the proof that life is fair is that both rich men and poor men get ice. The rich man gets his in the summer and the poor man in the winter. In the same way, the outhouse worked as a sauna and a freezer. You could sweat off weight in the summer and stick to the seat in the winter.

The water tank filled when you sat on the seat and flushed when you stood up. Childish ingenuity being what it is, and my being small enough to not be able to trip the plumbing device, I owned a pet rock heavy enough to make up the difference in weight. There I would sit, proud as any monarch on his throne, my pet rock on my lap—the king of all I beheld. All impediments overcome, I got to freeze and sweat just like the big guys. Funny what's important when your just a kid and don't know any better.

Chapter Thirty-Eight

All Day Sucker!

We always had all we needed and sometimes little extras. But like most greedy children, whose eyes were bigger than their bellies, we often wanted more than was good for us. I, for one, lusted for jaw breakers. In those days, and I don't know if it's still true, they sold candy in school at recess time. It seemed to be my unfortunate lot in life to never come out even with these coveted confections. Either I had money and they had no jaw breakers, or more often, they had an ample supply and I had no cash. At first, it was a minor annoyance, and then it became a psychosis. Let's face it; I was a jaw breaker junkie with no way to get a fix.

One fine day, while minding my own business and playing with my cousin in a vacant lot, there before my startled greedy little eyes, crumpled up in the scruffy grass and weeds, was a five dollar bill. Wow! My parents spent ten dollars a week for all of our groceries, and I had five dollars—the opportunity of a lifetime. First I had to, and was glad to, share with my cousin. Then there was a small stack of used comic books. Do you remember used comic books? They were sold with the top half of the cover torn off. They were five cents each, six for a quarter.

This still left more money than I ever had, or likely ever would have, to spend on jaw breakers. I had bags full of the wonderful little things. I had to go to three different grocery stores to buy that many. I hid my greedy little stash in my secret hideout, a cavernous hole behind some loose bricks in the wall in my backyard. The plan was perfect. For the rest of my natural life, I could go to my "goodie bank," say "open sesame," and fill my pockets with a day's supply. And so I did, for a little while anyhow. I would stop by my hoard and load up as I headed out for the day. With one pocket full of red and one pocket full of black, they quickly became a currency: a trade, a purchase, a bribe or a tip. I was flush and ready for all comers.

In addition to these goodies, my pockets carried the essentials of survival: a coin or two maybe, a couple of bottle caps, some marbles, a pocketknife, a small ball of string, a "neat" stone, and a few unidentified treasures that I found along the way. Thank God I never fell into deep water; there would have been no way to get me off the bottom. My reign was short and called on account of rain. Regrettably, the sun doesn't always shine. It began to rain, and it rained in biblical proportions. It was one of those three-day storms that soaked the whole world and my jaw breakers too, even ones in secret hiding places. The colors ran and the individual spheres became a massive lump, and I think something green was beginning to grow. Panic! What to do? What to do?

There was just one answer. It was early in the morning and I had all day to solve this sticky problem. The only thing to do was to eat them all. I got a good stack of comic books, climbed up onto my favorite rooftop hideout and began the prodigious task. What could be better? All my life I wanted jaw breakers and now I had them. Bags full and bags full and bags full, and nothing to do from breakfast 'till dinner but stuff one after another after another into my greedy little mouth. I had made an excuse why I wouldn't be home for lunch, which I often did. Nothing would interfere with this feast and nothing did. I ate and ate and ate.

By dinnertime, I had done my very best, but alas and alack, there were still bags full. And now I had a different problem. I no longer cared what became of my swag. My first problem was to get down off the roof and all the way home. I could barely stand, let alone walk or climb. It was very dicey whether I could get down before my goodies came up. Amid fits of sugar shock, with head spinning and stomach turning, on I pressed. Somehow or other I made it all that long way home. It was a tortured trip, to say the least. Now the problem was to explain why the little boy with the green face wanted no parts of dinner or anything else. As it turned out, I didn't have to explain anything. I guess the fact that both of my ends were going at the same time was a big hint. I was sick. My hair was sick, my toenails were sick, I was very, very sick. I lost every last one of those jaw breakers—the hard way. It was no fun at all. I believe I stopped just this side of turning completely inside out. I lived, I didn't want to, but I lived anyway. This was my punishment, no doubt, for my gluttony. To this day, if I think of the taste of jaw breakers, my stomach gets a little queasy and I get a bad taste in the back of my mouth. Be careful what you wish for, you just might get it.

Chapter Thirty-Nine

At one point, Judy, Miriam, and Donna slept in the same room. As will always be the case, when children are left to their own devices, they will invent games. Among the games invented by these three gentile little ladies was "Circus." This involved mostly acrobatic daring feats. While the two younger ones would lie side by side in the middle of the bed, the third performer would climb hundreds of feet in the air, all the way to the top of the chest of drawers. Then, without consideration for life and limb, the fearless young lady would dive, and at the very last second, the two faithful assistants would roll out of the way. The crowd cheered wildly. Their success with this death-defying act naturally led to many other tricks, and eventually led to one too many. One fine evening, while getting ready for bed, the big-time circus performer, Judy, tried to jump from the sink to the tub by swinging on the shower curtain rod. Now let me point out that my father had just finished redoing the bathroom including new wallpaper. Fact #1: Shower curtain rods were not meant to swing on. Fact #2: There is not enough time to come up with a good excuse while you're falling. Fact #3: It looks very suspicious to be sitting in a bathtub, fully dressed, with a curtain rod in your hands and the new wall-paper hanging down all over you. The circus left town that night, sadder but wiser.

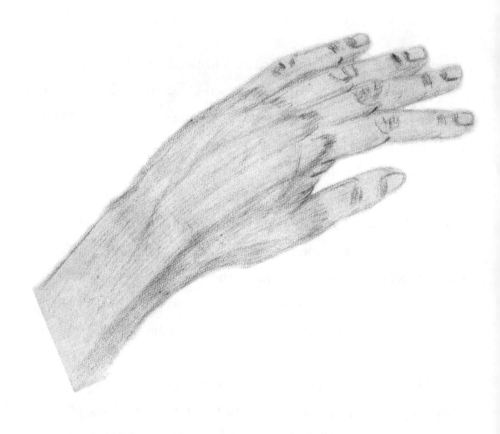

Chapter Forty

When meeting a friend, it's a hand we extend,
and when we touch it feels—
but as long as we live nothing finer we give,
than the touch of the hand that heals.

T.J.G.

Miriam is a nurse practitioner, a very learned and responsible position and a gentle, soft-spoken lady, who medically kicks butt. In her job she is charged with the health and well-being of a large number of seriously ill young people. In addition, whenever there is a health problem in our family, you can bet she is the first one to get a call. Her kindness and patience are amazing.

Not too bad for a kid who came here from outer space. I might have mentioned that sometimes the older ones picked on the younger ones. Miriam and a friend, a co-alien, would tell her poor baby sister that they had come here in a rocket ship and would soon have to go back. This was while playing in the park. This park was across the street from the home into which we had moved and was in a nicer area of the city. They would hear the call coming from the spaceship and begin to climb a park bench, as if they were floating away. When they had tortured their poor sister enough for the day, they would get a cancellation order, "for now anyway."

Another little torment, dreamed up by my sweet, fiendish little sister, to plague her little sister, was that she would tell Donna that she (Donna) had not been born into the family and that our Mom and Dad had found her in the sewer, and the law said she could only stay for awhile. When she turned twelve, she would have to go back. Why twelve? I don't know!

It sometimes wonders me, how we all grew up with a small semblance of sanity. It just goes to prove, that with a little luck and a lot of love, you can overcome anything, even six siblings. Survive we did, and thrive we did.

Donna grew up to be sane and a very nice lady to boot. She is the proud mother of two fine boys, worthy of her pride and of all of ours as well. Go Baby Sister!!!

To this day she mourns the fact that she has no memories of Bologna Row. She was born after we moved. Maybe this book will help her share our experiences and the memories they left. After all she's just a baby sister and all of this took place before she was here . . . and now you know, and she does too.

Chapter Forty-One

Cass is the elder statesperson of the clan and a natural-born big sister. She was always the little lady, neat, clean and very fussy. When she would dress for a date she was always the queen of clean. She didn't appreciate us soiled gremlins with jelly on our faces and peanut butter on our hands. She didn't really understand just how messy hands could get. As if to prove that God has a good sense of humor Cass had five kids. She spent a good deal of her time up to her armpits in dirty diapers. In fact she used to say "when the youngest was potty trained, she would make a planter out of the diaper pail." Her children were about the funniest kids the Good Lord ever made. Over the years I've enjoyed telling and retelling the stories of their exploits. They once, after seeing paste wax used, helped their mom by waxing the kitchen floor, with Crisco. If anyone should write a book, it's Cass; her kids gave her an almost endless supply of great stories. They are living proof that no matter how active, adventurous, and imaginative children are, with a little love and a point in the right direction, they will turn out just fine. They are, in fact, some of the nicer people I've ever known. Being in their company is a little like a visit to my youth. I love to watch them interact with each other and to listen to their stories. It's a lot like when my sisters and I get together. A family is a wonderful thing, and this I do know.

Chapter Forty-Two

One of my sister Floss' friends has been a dear friend since they sat next to each other in first grade. I've said that life was simpler, less complicated, less involved in those bygone days, but that's not always true. A big deal back then was, on a Saturday night, to go to the corner drugstore for a Coke and to play the jukebox. That's the simple part.

After dinner my sister would leave the house to meet her friend. A few minutes later that friend would show up at our front door. "Is Floss here?" she asked. "No, she left to meet you," we told her. "Ok," and with that she was gone. A few minutes later, Floss would appear again, poking her head in the door, looking for her friend. "Is she here?" "Nope, she's been and gone," we would tell her. "Thank you." And with that she vanished into the night for the next round. There were always several near misses before they would finally link up. Meantime, my father would be watching this show and laughing uproariously. He called them Brenda & Cobenia . . . why? I don't know . . . she just used to say things like that. The rest of us loved to watch him watching them, and we laughed uproariously. We loved to laugh and still do, with or without good reason. It's funny the things we laugh at. Sometimes, when you try to retell something that was really funny at the time, it doesn't seem funny again. I guess you just had to be there. I'm sure glad that I was.

Floss has three children; two girls and a boy. The girls are now pretty ladies and great moms like their mom. The young man, also grown up and newly married, is a history major and one of the most interesting people to talk to.

Chapter Forty-Three

My Dad died from a heart attack. He was much too young and we still miss him. He is still with us at family gatherings with all his sayings and stories. He was just naturally funny without trying to be, and usually didn't realize it himself. Whether he was scolding us, telling a funny story, or just talking at the dinner table, he had a whole cast of characters to help make his point. Characters like Hogan's goat, Mickey the dunce, and Tom Pepper, who got thrown out of Hell for lying. Those were some of his favorites. He would bring them up at the oddest times, while making a serious point and it was up to us not to laugh. He also had an endless store of witty little rhymes and sayings. He could regale us with tales of his youth and his many friends and associates *i.e.,* "The Loyal Sons of the Beach." He used to tell us he had been for a swim over to Ireland to have a "brick fight." We were never sure where the tales ended and the tall tales began, and it really didn't matter. His stories were great fun and still make us laugh.

Chapter Forty-Four

Sleep dear one, in fields of flowers,
Heedless of the fleeting hours.
For time gone by, and time to be,
Are at last as one to thee.

T.J.G.

Growing up, Rita and I were close. We were close in age and close in temperament. We had many fine adventures and countless Saturday afternoon movie matinees. She grew up to be the mother of five great kids—children who now miss their mom. Rita died of breast cancer, a fate I wouldn't wish on the devil himself. Please get regular check-ups and take the time and trouble to stay on top of this. The alternative is not acceptable.

Chapter Forty-Five

One fine Saturday, my cousin and I, as we often did, went to a movie at one of the local theaters. Sometimes, not often, they would advertise one movie, and for whatever reason, show something else. Usually they would make an announcement and offer a refund. This particular theater was infamous for pulling a switch and pretending nothing had happened. This was bad enough, but to top it off, the movie they *did* show was a real "stinker." I was angry and wanted to leave, but my cousin insisted on staying through the entire show and the beginning of the next one. I should have suspected there was a plot hatching. As the substitute movie began to play, my cousin slipped out of the seat and quietly up onto the stage. There, in a loud stage voice, making the announcement of how we had come to see a different and better movie, then launched into a tirade of how unfair this was, and how often it happened. Continuing with a complete rundown on the plot of the movie, and how it ended. Somewhere during the process, the ushers had moved in to put an end to this insurrection. Their problem was that they had stage fright and were too timid to charge up there and to do the deed. Meanwhile, in an attempt to avoid capture, my cousin had begun to improvise a tap dance. Now the bad plot had turned into a movie musical being sung and danced in voice and pantomime. I was laughing so hard, I had tears in my eyes and a pain in my side. The funniest thing was the effect all of this had on the rest of the audience. It would be normal if they were annoyed at the disruption and angry at hearing the plot and ending of the movie, but this couldn't have been further from the truth. As I looked around, the crowd was reacting just like me. They were literally rolling in the aisles, stomping their feet, and crying from laughing so hard. Eventually, even the ushers got the joke and sat on the floor laughing. Whereupon my cousin, with the mission accomplished, beat a hasty retreat out the side door, with me in hot pursuit. As we made our way from the cool, dark, pandemonium of the theater, to the bright quiet heat of the summer sidewalk, we were aware that the full house, acting as a single individual, was standing and cheering. We laughed a fall-down, slap-your-thigh kind of laugh all the way home. We were never quite sure whether they had cheered for what was done or because we were leaving. Thereafter we restricted our patronage to other movie houses. There were plenty to choose from.

Chapter Forty-Six

My very earliest memory is being in a crib and looking out between the bars. The crib was in my parents' bedroom. On the bureau was a camera. Not a regular box camera, but a camera with a collapsing lens, like a professional camera, but smaller. It was chrome with tan leather panels and trim. It was sitting there opened and staring at me while I stared back at it. I'm not at all sure whether or not I was frightened by it, I just remember looking at it in amazement, and it looking at me the same way. I found out years later that it was a German camera that had been sent home from overseas by one of my uncles. To me, it was a great wonder and just a little scary. It made such an impression on me at such an early age that if I closed my eyes to this day, I can see it clearly. It was a strong beginning for a growing store of memories of those terrible and wonder-filled war years. It sometimes amazes me that I remember so much from that time so long ago, yet I can't remember what time church is on Sunday. I think maybe it has to do with how important events were, and maybe I sensed this in the people around me. Whatever it was, I wouldn't trade my memories for a bag of gold. Well, not a small bag anyway. But then again . . . I'm just a kid, so what do I know?

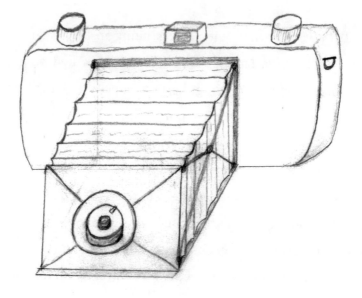

Chapter Forty-Seven

It's strange how the mind works. There are things that I remember that I clearly remember. There are things that I remember that I probably don't. There are stories that I've heard so often that my mind thinks it remembers them, but a lot of the details have been filled in by others. This is a story that I think I remember, surely parts of it I do, but I was so young at the time that it's hard to believe. Whoever the memory comes from, it involves a time when I was just starting to get around on my own.

Back in those days, the thinking was that toddlers needed to wear strong support shoes. They looked like clodhoppers. They were brown high-top shoes with high arches and laced above the ankle. With very little alteration they could have served as football or soccer boots. My Mom, being my Mom, kept them clean and well-polished. There was, however, no way to gild this lily. The size of them, on my rather small person, made them appear to be eating my legs from the foot up. Thusly well anchored, I toddled into the world. Klomp . . . klomp . . . klomp.

It wasn't too long before my parents realized something was very wrong. I had begun to walk like the "lone cowhand from the

Rio Grande." When I jumped, instead of landing on my feet, I pulled them up and landed on my knees. It didn't seem to matter to me if I was jumping on the living room floor or on the brick sidewalk. Clearly I was having a problem. A trip to the doctor confirmed this fact. However, after stating the obvious, the doctor could offer no further help. He suggested we see a specialist. Now I know that today this would be no big thing, we go to a specialist for everything. But, at that time, it was a big deal—big and expensive. My poor father turned pale at the thought of paying for a doctor who could have an office on Parkside Ave. Today, this is a rundown area of the city, but back then it was considered "elite." I remember riding out there on the "trolley car." It was one of the old-fashioned trolley cars with the front of the car at both ends. In the middle was a compartment for the conductor to help collect fares. The backs of all of the seats switched back and forth like a toggle, so the passengers could face the front in either direction and the entire thing was made of wood. The hand straps were made of ridged iron and were covered with white porcelain. There was a large loud bell on which the trolley driver rang a bright and lively tune at every large cross street. I thoroughly enjoyed the entire excursion, my poor father, on the other hand, spent his time worrying about diagnoses and doctor bills, etc. When we at last arrived, after a moderate purgatory in the waiting room, we were ushered into the main office. I remember thinking that with all the chrome and porcelain and charts and pictures, this looks like the kind of a place Dr. Frankenstein would like to hang out. Stripped to my underwear, which, by the way, was clean and void of all unplanned holes, I was checked out. I was measured and examined from my nose to my toes. I sat on a very cold metal table and, albeit painlessly, assaulted by many and various calipers and something that looked like the thing they use in a shoe store. (Except that he used it on my arms and legs.) After measuring all of my muscles and bones and noting the results on a pad with a body drawn on it, he then spent what seemed a long time going over his notes and doing a considerable number of "harrumphs." He looked up and made his pronouncement. The doctor, a large man with a deep and impressive voice, said, "Sir . . . (dramatic pause) . . . throw out those stupid clodhoppers and buy the boy a pair of moccasins, and when the weather permits, let him go barefoot."

It seems I have a slight peculiarity, an extra muscle in my arch and it's covered by a fat pad. This serves as a cushion that I walk on. Result, for me, good shoes are bad and bad shoes are great. Go figure! No medicines! No treatments! No deformity! No disease!

Then, on top of all of this good news, the kind doctor must have felt sorry for us. He charged us little or nothing for all the time he had spent, he said I was very interesting. Interesting is good, for a skinny little kid from Bologna Row.

My relieved, grateful, and happy father took my Mom and me to a fancy ice cream parlor in Fairmount Park. It was a neat old place with wire and cane chairs and little tables with marble tops. They served enormous sundaes with real whipped cream and cherries on the top, big glasses of ice water with little handles on the side, and red and white striped straws. Then at last, with stomachs full to the brim, we mounted one of those beautiful old trolley cars for the long trip home. Tired, contented, and at peace with the world, Bologna Row looked great. And even though I was just a kid, I remember. At least I think I do.

While I'm thinking of doctors, do you remember when doctors made house calls? We had a family doctor we called Doctor Pat. His real name was long and very Italian. We kids could never have pronounced it, so, he was Doctor Pat. A kindly old gentleman with a very waxed mustache that looked like the letter "V." He had a big round face, wreathed with a large, jovial smile. When he came to the house everybody got an examination. I remember being lined up at the kitchen table in our underwear. When there was an epidemic of mumps, chicken pox, or whatever hit the neighborhood, he would even have us bring in other kids. As a reward for good behavior there was always a generous stash of lollipops from his mysterious black bag. This bottomless treasure trove held an endless supply of not only goodies but medical necessaries as well. Almost anything he needed was somewhere in that bag. There were bottles of medicine and jars of pills. Concoctions with mysterious names: Spirits of Sweet Niter, oil of camphor, boric acid, cod liver oil, Coke syrup, Epsom salts, peppermint oil and on and on—the list had no end. My favorite was a mixture of Niter and warm sugar water, which we got for fevers. I remember liking the taste of it. On occasion there was even a large and unpleasant hypodermic needle, not the little plastic kind you see now. This one was a big, chrome and glass thing that he boiled on the stove and reused until the point was only a distant memory. But, since he was there, all medical needs were met on the kitchen table. He charged not by the patient, but by the visit, a tribute to his dedication and a boon to our economy. In that long ago era, doctors were very different. Health care, like so many things, had a different meaning; the care part seemed so much more important. Then again . . . I was just a kid so what did I know? But, I still think I remember.

Chapter Forty-Eight

School was a big deal. I'm not sure I was ready for it, nor it for me. My poor Dad was called to school so often, I think he got an attendance award. I had difficulty with most subjects, spending a great deal of time looking out the window and wishing for summer. I was not very good in any subject, and I was bad in most. The exception was math. (In math, I was horrendous.) I never understood the concept of math. I always thought that you had to just know the answers. I wasn't quite sure how . . . but you had to know them. I could see no other possible way to figure it out. Problem: Dick and Jane boarded a train in Philadelphia and traveled at 60 miles per hour, how much did they pay for lunch? What?! I'd sit there while other children shouted answers . . . some right . . . some wrong . . . but answers. I hadn't a clue. I would sneak looks at other kids' books, thinking they must have answers printed in them. Just my luck, I got a defective book! Finally, I was reduced to outright "fakery." While the rest of the kids, with their little hands raised and waving in the air, shouted out answers, I would raise my hand and move my lips making nary a sound, but lip-syncing for all the world to see . . . like I knew what I was doing. I was in high school before I really understood numbers. A teacher had a ruler with a zero in the middle and numbers ascending and descending in each direction. It was as if a curtain was parted. I understood how numbers were related, and how you could figure out the answer. No longer was math a foreign language. One subject down, and the rest to go. I'm still a poor reader. I love to read. I understand and remember what I read. I am laboriously slow and must work at sounding out words. As for spelling? Well, I have a theory: before babies are born, God lines them all up and decrees, "You can spell, you can spell, you can't." Well, I'm a "you can't." As is the usual case, my handwriting has suffered from my poor spelling. I find that most "you can'ts" write the first letter of a word then sort of scribble a squiggly line and hope for the best. The reader gets to guess what it was supposed to be and entertain themselves by figuring out how it was spelled. It works for me. One thing that being a poor student gave me was a sense of humor. I found early on, that no one can laugh and give you a bad time at the same time. So, if you make a good enough joke you get off the hook for a little while anyhow. Unlearned and barely literate, I joked my way through nine of the first twelve years of school. When I finally began to learn as an adult I really enjoyed it. Imagine my amazement. I enjoyed geography, history, reading, math, science, and the whole curriculum. But I still can't spel.

Chapter Forty-Nine

Confessions of a failed student accepted and excepted, I started out well . . . well, well-dressed anyway. To start school, I had two new pair of knickers—a green pair and a brown pair. They were made of stiff corduroy. They were great! They made a whistling noise when you walked as your legs rubbed together. When you combine this with a new pair of shoes that squeaked when you walked, and topped it all off with an awful noise that I called whistling (a high-pitched screech caused by passing air through the space where a tooth used to be) I was a fine spectacle—a regular one-man band, full of himself and not much else. I was thoroughly pleased with my loud little self and quite ready to take on the world. Unfortunately, things went downhill from there. Homework was another bone of contention, and like two dogs fighting over a bone, the bone never wins. Whatever gray hairs my father had, I gave him from doing homework with me. If I had worked as hard at doing it as I did at getting out of it, I would have been a much better scholar. (I sound just like my father.) Once, while learning to define and spell vocabulary words, the word was "fodder" which I defined as the guy that married "mudder." Even my poor, tired father had to laugh—a decidedly infrequent event during our nightly trials. I think my Dad must have spent a lot of time looking out the window and wishing for summer too.

Chapter *Fifty*

I don't remember two of my grandparents. The two I do remember were my Dad's mom, an old lady, sick and bedridden, and my Mom's dad, a man of unlimited promise—a promise he never kept. He had many talents and abilities, but these gifts went unused because he drank. The one talent he did use was the great ability to empty bottles, too much and too often. He came up short as a husband and a father, but as a grand pop I kind of liked the old boy. He had some strange ways; but he was always good to me. He had a set of false teeth which he didn't often use because they bothered him. In lieu of teeth, he used a hand-cranked grinder. Into this magic appliance he would put all sorts of stuff, and when it came out, he covered it with blackstrap molasses and pronounced it a meal. It always seemed to me a wonder that he survived this mess. He not only survived but thrived. He could sleep on the front step on the coldest day in winter. He would sit on his frozen perch, read a newspaper, smoke his pipe, and fall asleep. Nothing seemed to bother him, not even his pipe which smelled bad enough to chase buzzards. His pipe tobacco started life as a cigar, a cheap cigar; I mean six for a quarter cheap cigars, which he smoked down to the nub. He would then chew the end. After that, he would dry the cob on the windowsill. They looked like horse droppings and smelled worse. When they were sufficiently dry, he would dice them up with an old rusty pocketknife and smoke them in his pipe. Between this and a little applejack wine, it is no wonder he was impervious. That combination would tan leather. For the latter part of his life he may not have been alive, just well preserved. He had strange ways, but as I said, he was always good to me. I remember once wanting very badly a set of frontier guns. They were each about two inches long and mounted on cardboard. The whole set cost the princely sum of twenty-five cents. I was moaning and groaning, and lamenting the fact that, "I can NEVER get anything I want". Later, when no one else was around, he slipped me a quarter, and told me to keep it under my hat. It wasn't the money. It wasn't the toy. It was a kindness quietly done. When he passed away, I didn't get to go to his funeral. He didn't have much of a funeral. I remember waking up that morning, knowing what was going on, and that I was missing it. We children had been left at home with an aunt. We dressed quickly. I dressed in dungarees, sneakers, and a striped polo shirt— a great outfit for a funeral. We sneaked out of the house and ran all the way to the funeral home. We arrived just as they were bringing the casket out to go to the cemetery. My Mom spotted us coming, and sent us home. I still wish I had gone to his funeral. He used to take great joy in teaching me things; how to sharpen a knife, how to cook kidneys with onions, and a lot more useful stuff. I wish he had had the time to teach me more. He was a bit of a scallywag, but I missed him all the same.

Chapter Fifty-One

Our little house on Bologna Row was every bit a small brick box. There was a basement with a low ceiling, bare rock walls and a dirt floor. There was a coal bin and a small coal furnace. I am being very generous in calling it a coal furnace. In fact, it burned everything and anything unwanted. There was very little, other than ash, that made it to the refuse. Most things in that distant age were made of metal, cloth, paper or wood, three out of four made it to the ashes. For all the things that ended their existence like Sam McGee or a Hindu Suttee, that hungry fire took in a lot more than it put out in heat. This was especially true early on a winter morning. My father spent most of his mornings trying to coax heat out of the furnace and into the house. As I said, the house resembled a box, with two square bedrooms upstairs, and downstairs there were two square rooms, a parlor, and a kitchen. Running on a diagonal from lower right to upper left, in between the rooms, was a staircase. At the bottom of the stairs was a large black iron heat register. This was the only source of heat in the house. In the winter, we kids, wrapped in blankets, would stand on this register to get dressed for school. Talk about growing up close.

On a cold day, that heat register would get hot enough to melt crayons. You ask how I know this. It was fun, for some reason, to watch crayons distort, dissolve and drip. It also got hot enough to burn your feet. It was always socks and shoes first while doing a little dance. Once dressed, and warm on the outside, there was a steaming bowl of oatmeal to warm the inside. On a cold winter day I love the smell of a fresh wood fire and the taste of a hot bowl of oatmeal. They still warm my heart and comfort my soul and for an all too brief instant I am, again, a little kid getting ready for school.

Chapter Fifty-Two

I may have told you, we lived next door to our cousins. A long-standing family joke, and the source of much teasing, was the ongoing conversation between my aunt and my Mom over the back fence. We used to say they couldn't talk to each other without that darned fence. Other than a conversational armrest, that fence served as a fort during Indian raids and a castle when the Vikings attacked. It was a mountain to scale and as many more things as there were days of play in that backyard. This included any day there wasn't a load of wash hanging on the line. The wash would hang in rows as neat and orderly as the neighborhoods themselves and hung by size and by color and with no "dog ears." If we helped, we had to do it the same way, or re-do it until it was perfect. Heaven forbid the wash would be disorderly, what would people think? At the very least, it would have made the evening newspaper. Maybe if a foreigner saw it, there would have been an international incident. Perhaps it was important because it didn't matter. My father's voice echoes endlessly in my head:

> *"If a task is once begun,*
> *Never leave it, till it's done.*

Be a task great or small,

Do it well or not at all."

- Unknown

Growing up, I thought this was something my father made up and I was shocked when I found this rhyme in a book, attributed to "Unknown." Maybe this was my Dad's *"nom de plume."*

Chapter Fifty-Three

Another great taboo was that if you went anywhere, especially out of the neighborhood, you absolutely had to wear clean underwear with no holes in them. God forbid you should go to a hospital and not have clean underwear. The doctors would immediately throw you out onto the sidewalk. Not only this, but the entire city would stop, cluck, and ask what kind of parents you must have. Whatever kind of an accident you could have could not be as bad as having a hole in your sock. It sounds silly in this day and age of people dressing as sloppily as they can, but back then you took pride in how you looked and in all you did. It reflected on your family. This pride in how you looked was confirmed for me many years later. My wife and I were advisors for our church's youth group. We, along with the other advisors, had decided to try something different with the kids. At that time, sloppy was in style: jeans with holes in the knees, old and poor-fitting shirts, dirty white sneakers, etc. So we planned a formal dance with boutonnières for the boys and corsages for the girls. The parish hall had fancy decorations and a photo booth—the whole nine yards. We even had fancy food, which I noticed no one was eating. Knowing the way these kids could eat, I panicked, something must be wrong with the food. I sidled up to a group of the boys and asked, out of the side of my mouth, in my best imitation of a grade "B" prison movie, "What's wrong with the food?" "Nothing Mr. 'G', but you can't 'pig out' when you're dressed this nice," he said. The Snowball dance became an annual affair, but with a little less food and even more ambiance. Clothes cannot only make the man or woman, but can help to give him or her pride in how they look and who they are. Just a thought, in case you're a kid who doesn't know any better, try dressing nicely, it makes you feel nice.

Chapter Fifty-Four

There were certain people that you just didn't argue with or sass because their authority was without question. This included priests, ministers, rabbis, policemen, politicians, teachers, doctors, lawyers, and Indian chiefs. They knew it all, and like Santa, they had a list of everything we did naughty or nice, and so did most of the neighbors. That was one of the not so good things about living in a "small" neighborhood. When you did something that you weren't supposed to do, chances were very good that someone saw you, and that they knew your folks. School teachers also knew everything and they had their own language to describe it. In the language of the schools, if you misbehaved you weren't just being bad you were a "Bold Brazen Article." If you had trash on your desk, you were told to get that "Truck" off of your desk. I was often told to stop skylarking. (I'm not sure what this was, but apparently I was good at it.) If, or should I say, when you got into trouble in school, it was noted on your "permanent record" which follows you for the rest of your life. It would be nice, in today's world, if anything were permanent, even your record, instead of being disposable. I sometimes think that the world won't end—

it'll just get thrown away. I'm quite sure the only reason my permanent record isn't still following me, like a pet dog, is that it's so large and so full of bad marks that no one can lift it. Somewhere in the universe sits my permanent record awash in red ink. Oh well!

What did I know? I was just a kid.

Chapter Fifty-Five

I remember block parties. Not the elaborate expensive things with rented Ferris wheels, these were more impromptu affairs. The main ingredients were: a record player, a stack of records, a big pot of hot dogs and some sauerkraut, a little liquid refreshment, some red-white-and-blue crepe paper and a string of party lights. Last, but not least, a homemade stand where you could pitch pennies to win a bowl you didn't want. The bowls were tan in color with an iridescent finish. Look in the back of the cupboard or a corner of the attic and you probably have one. They were everywhere. So were block parties. It seemed to me as if there was a party going on somewhere in the area at all times during the summer. From far away you could see the crowds and hear the music. We loved those block parties because we got to stay up 'till all hours, singing, dancing and carrying on. Even after we were trundled off to bed, we would sneak into my parents' room and peak out of the window to watch the goings on. There really wasn't much to see, but whatever there was, we didn't want to miss it. We watched until our eyes were heavy and wanted to close. Then we lay in bed and watched the shadows on the walls and ceilings that were cast by the strings of party lights. Long, funny shadow people on the walls and ceiling were dancing like long-legged spiders. It became difficult to tell the difference between awake and asleep, between reverie and dreams. Music, dreams, voices, and shadows were swirling inside our little heads, all misty and mixed together. There we floated somewhere between the real and unreal worlds, neither awake nor asleep, but dreaming the dreams our imaginations painted . . . block parties.

Chapter Fifty-Six

Sometime shortly after the war, my uncles, like all the "lucky" G.I.'s, were coming home. One of my uncles, with his mustering out pay, bought a car. He was one of, if not the first person I knew personally, who owned a car. He called it the "Green Hornet." It had plenty of seating room, but the neatest seat of all was the "rumble seat." I don't quite understand why, but riding in that rumble seat was just about the coolest thing I had ever done in my entire life. To help celebrate the occasion we took a ride to the seashore. When I say "we," I mean all of us, everyone I knew, and some I didn't know. I don't know the exact number, but there were bodies everywhere in that big, fine car. Now I tell you, life was very different then, and so was everything in it. There were no super highways and no expressways, there was just mile after mile of dirt roads—dirt roads and cow paths. The dirt road we chose was just wide enough for one car and had corn growing on either side. Long about one and a half hours into our little adventure, I ask the dumb question that everyone else was thinking, "What do we do if a car comes the other way?" whereupon my father advised, in a harsh and hurried voice, "Be quiet!" For once in my young and impetuous life, I took the hint. No problem! All that long, long way down to the shore, and back home again, and we never saw another car. When I think back and remember how far you could ride and never see a house, a car, or even a store, I realize how very different life was when I was young. And yes, I didn't know any differently or how much I should have appreciated it because: "I was just a Kid."

Chapter Fifty-Seven

More on the story of the funny little car from Bologna Row. (COUPE, pronounced "coop" as in chicken, from the French, for small car with too many kids in it.)

My Dad's first car was a nineteen-thirty something Plymouth Coupe. A coupe was that era's version of a two-door compact car. I don't believe the overall size was that much different from other cars. Most of the difference was in the passenger compartment. It had a small front seat and an even smaller back seat. With a gang like ours, we had to improvise. Once the rear seat was removed, there was seating from just behind the front seat all the way back to the trunk. On long trips, we sat on our luggage; all and all not too uncomfortable. Seat belts? What are they? They use them in airplanes . . . don't they?

The car was black with a white stripe on either side. Naturally, we called it "the skunk." When I think of the age and condition of that car, I can't get over their nerve. To pile that many kids into that old rattletrap and go the places we went . . . well, at the very least, it is a tribute to their faith. Maybe we just didn't know any better, but we always had unlimited faith that things would work out, and they seemed to do just that. I remember one Christmas going shopping with my parents. When I say "shopping," you may think of going to a chain store in a mall. Well, not quite. This shopping took place in a big metal building, a real bargain outlet. They had lots of "one of a kinds" and "nearly perfect" items which they auctioned off to the highest bidder. But, they had plenty of good toys cheap, so there we shopped. It was well out of the way on an old dirt road that was two cars wide and riddled with pot holes. The weather was raw and cold with a slight rain that should have been snow. Later, fog came—the kind of a fog that belonged in a Sherlock Holmes movie. You couldn't see the front end of the car. Undeterred, we stayed later and bought more than we should have. When at last we headed home, in our little car with no heat, we must have been a sight to see. There was my father driving, as best he could, my mother praying, and she was good at it, and me hanging out of the window, trying to navigate, and all of us were wrapped in blankets. My job was to try to keep us close to the side of the road. With red ears and bleary eyes, I stayed at my post all the way home. A trip that should have been forty-five minutes or an hour lasted several torturous hours of hair-raising adventure. Now you may think this would have scared us off, but not a bit. It wasn't long before we were off on another shopping adventure. We had a gang of kids, and if they had bargains we were there. Damn the torpedoes . . . full speed ahead. Christmas is coming, the geese are getting fat . . . etc. . . . etc. . . . etc. . . .

Chapter Fifty-Eight

Road Games

Whenever we went on a car trip, like most other families, we played road games. My favorite was "license plates." The object of this game was to see, and note, as many plates from as many states as possible. Unlike today, there were no vanity plates, no commemoratives and special plates honoring the passing of the passenger pigeon, etc. Each state had its own colors and shape and almost never varied. You could spot and identify a license plate a lot further away than you could read the name on it. Unbeknownst to me, I was actually learning lot of things . . . and I just thought I was having fun. When we first began to play the game, we had a map, pencil, and paper. As I became better at the game, I could keep the map in my head. I began to know the names and shapes of all forty-eight states. It seems the more you use your brain the better it operates. I must admit, I still play the game, and now I have added the wrinkle of using it as a memory exercise as well. I can go on a trip, keep the map in my brain, and color in the states as I see them. I arrive at my destination, enjoy whatever delights it has to offer, and pick up the game where I left off on the return trip. I can look at the map in my head and see states that I had forgotten and that I had already seen. I do individual states, and then move to areas like New England, Mid-Atlantic, etc. I use different colors for each. I learned a lot of geography and had a lot of fun. I highly recommend this silly children's game. It's good for you and it's fun. Maybe you could learn a little, too, even if you're not a kid.

Chapter Fifty-Nine

Sometimes, during the long hot summers, in the early evenings, after supper, and before bedtime, the heat would own the rest of the day. Since there were no air conditioners, no televisions, no internet, and not even a window fan, (at least we never owned one), there was no escape. Amidst the pleasant odors that remembered dinner, the heat of the day hung heavy in the air. Inside the house was worse, but not much. At least outside there was the occasional breeze. Often on such nights, while small family groups sat on their front steps, one of the older boys would magically appear with hydrant wrench in hand. The younger kids would play in the stream of water, quietly at first, and then a bucket would come out to play. "Water fight alert!" After everyone was thoroughly wet and the water wars died down, the moms stepped in and took charge of the buckets, and with brooms in hand, cleaned everything in sight, walls, steps, and sidewalks . . . everything got cleaned . . . don't stand too still for too long, you'll get the cleaning of your young life. Soon the hydrant was turned off and the busy activities came to a halting stop. As things quieted, the adults gathered in small knots. A cup of coffee or a glass of beer and a soft conversa-

tion with short bursts of laughter were here and there. The hot air hung heavy everywhere but now with the smell of fresh and clean like after a summer shower. Meanwhile, kids gathered in the same kind of small knots, imitating the adults. We sat on the steps playing quietly and trying hard not to attract attention. If they didn't notice us, they wouldn't send us to bed—the bane of all childhood. Eventually, no matter how well-behaved we were, the moms, one by one, rounded up their brood and herded them off to bed leaving only the men. The men sat on the steps, still in small clusters, enjoying whatever breeze there might be, and smoked their pipes and cigars perfuming the summer air with their own sweet, smoky odors. The heat wasn't any less, but somehow it wasn't as troubling in that comfortable setting. Just to sit on the cool marble steps and talk, and laugh with the other children, was calming and made you feel cooler and a little more prepared for the moms' roundup. When we were finally able to settle down we fell asleep to the soft murmur of familiar voices outside the window, or maybe a quiet radio inside and the summer heat everywhere.

I remember one such summer night in particular. It was a hot muggy night. The humidity hung in the air so densely that you almost believed that if you were to jump in the air, you would be able to swim. It had been raining for the better part of a week. My Dad had just finished putting new wallpaper up in the back bedroom. I note this fact because my Dad had a singular talent for decorating just before a disaster. Unbeknownst to my poor, decorating Dad, there was a small leak in the roof, and several days worth of rain had accumulated on top of the ceilings. Somewhere between ten-thirty and eleven o'clock at night, when we kids were all in a good sound sleep, without warning, and with a loud roar, down came the soggy ceiling. Instant pandemonium! My Dad came bounding up the steps, two at a time, as fast as he could. As fast as he was moving, he was slow compared to the dog. At that time we had a large, black female dog named Jingles. She was a good, protective, and motherly dog. There she was, hip deep in rubble, barking and digging, rescuing kids and cleaning their faces. There were a few bumps and bruises but no real injuries. Other than a big mess to clean up, all was well once again on Bologna Row.

Chapter Sixty

Do you remember sitting in church in the summertime? Air-conditioners consisted of a holy picture, with an advertisement for a funeral parlor on the back, stapled to a tongue depressor. The only places I remember that had real air-conditioners were movie theaters and department stores. When my Mom had to do some hard-core shopping she would sometimes take me along. She said it was to help her, but I think it was to prevent me from getting into trouble. I had a slight tendency to get into mischief. "Tubbed and scrubbed and dressed to the nines" we hopped on the "El" and went downtown. Center city was a maze of department stores. Unfortunately, most of them no longer exist. They have gone along with Bobby Socks and Zoot Suits. Another thing that is sadly gone from the American scene is the H & H Automat. My mother shamelessly used the automat as bribery. If I was well-behaved and didn't act like a total itch, we would eat lunch at the automat. What a wonderful place. For a small handful of nickels you could eat like a king. Prowling around with the keys to the kingdom I could get anything I wanted for one or two nickels. It was delicious, nutritious and plenty. Not burger and fries but a plethora (how do you like that word?) of goodies: creamed spinach, baked beans, stewed tomatoes, home fried potatoes, Swiss steak, macaroni and cheese, and on and on. The list was almost without end. This was real fast food, not unidentified frying objects, but good food fast. Burger joints are new, but all that is new is not progress.

Chapter Sixty-One

This is very true . . . all that is new is not progress, but some things are. Shortly after the war, I heard about computers on the radio. At that time, a computer consisted of a large room full of vacuum tubes, a couple thousand miles of wire, and God only knows what else. All of this, and it was only a glorified adding machine. It's sometimes difficult for a person my age to get hold of things that move so fast. In my lifetime we have moved from getting phone calls at the corner store to cell phones and PC's. When I tell my grandchildren that most people didn't have a phone in their home they think I'm kidding. A phone call, if you got one, was very important and was never for "chit-chat." Someone would call the local candy store, if it had a public phone, and for a small tip one of the kids would run and tell you that you had a call. Then it was up to you to get to the store and answer the phone. For all their problems, cell phones are progress. My grandchildren can't imagine life without videos, cell phones, computers, answering machines and all the rest of the modern technology. They are kind, patient, and willing to help the old guy when he doesn't understand. Bravely they sail into the future—dragging Pop-Pop like an intellectual sea anchor. Just think, they're only kids, how smart will they be when they grow up?

Chapter Sixty-Two

Sometimes, in the dog days of summer, when vacation was over and school had not yet started, and there was nothing interesting to do, the days seemed to start early, move slowly, and end late. To fight the boredom, my cousin and I explored the neighborhood rooftops. We seemed to spend a considerable amount of time on rooftops. Why? Because we were nine years old and we could. Now it may seem strange to you that we played on rooftops. But if we had lived in the country, life would have been a little different. There we would have been barefoot and cheeks of tan, spending our time climbing apple trees, and looking for all the world like a Norman Rockwell painting. Too bad for us, we lived on a small street in the heart of the city, where there were no apple trees, so we did our climbing on roofs. A rooftop in the heat of summer has a smell all its own, never to be mistaken for cologne, but pleasant in its own way. I don't remember doing anything special up there. It was just the challenge of getting and being up there. Maybe there was something about perching high above life. This particular day I found a light bulb. "AH HA" . . . a hand grenade. I reared back and let it fly. Gee, it seemed like such a good idea at the time. There was, unknown to me, a small round hole in the glass bulb. It sliced my hand like a sharp knife through a ripe tomato. Ever the astute one, I quickly came to the realization that I was knee deep in the hurt locker. How do I get down from the roof? How do I get home? How do I get help? Never fear, my cousin was here! Never lost for an idea, my cousin quickly produced an old pair of dark blue or faded purple cloth gloves. Wadded up and used as medical packing, they stemmed the flow of blood and acted as padding. Let's not talk about the sanitation of this padding or even think about the pocket they came from. Let's, instead, talk about how to climb down from our perch with my little fist balled up, holding the dirty gloves in place. Somehow, after days and days of climbing, with constant help and guidance, I reached the bottom of Mt. Everest, still alive and halfway home. The second half of the journey, although not as perilous, was every bit as slow and painful as the first.

When I finally reached home, I dramatically fell in the front door, like a wounded movie hero home from the wars. Now it was my poor mother's job. She was amazingly cool and purposeful like it was an everyday occurrence. She held me up with one hand and worked feverishly with the other. Wipe away the blood, clean up the wound, apply a somewhat cleaner dressing, and hold it in place to stop the bleeding. She made arrangements with someone to watch the other kids and took me to the hospital for stitches. This may sound simple; but not so. First, it involved washing hands and faces and changing clothes. There were no phones, no cars, and no men. They were all away at work. It was entirely on her. Off she started, wounded pup in tow. Walking two blocks to the avenue to get a trolley car, transfer to the trolley that went to the front of the hospital, dismount our trusty, if not convenient, transport, and drag me inside for shots and stitches. Then, having no money, she had to make arrangements to pay the bill. That was no small feat in that day and age. Then we had to repeat the process in reverse to get home in time to make dinner and to catch up on the work she missed. Some fun eh kid! Thank God I wasn't twins. When I asked her later how she ever managed, she would only say that she had grown up with a lot of brothers, a mom that had to work, and that she had been through the same thing before. Knowing my uncles, I'm sure she was in that same spot many times . . . many times.

Chapter Sixty-Three

It's my fish and I'll fry if I want to!

As a youngster, I had an aunt who was just old enough to be a big person and still young enough to be a lot of fun. She took me places, bought me things, and generally spoiled me royally. One summer, when I was very young, we were all at the seashore, family and extended family together. She took me fishing at the local harbor, my first ever such trip. I remember, in turns, being first excited, then bored and then excited again. It's tough for a little kid to just sit and wait for a fish to bite on your line. So after a little while I got bored and started to lose interest in the project. My aunt began to focus my attention with tales of all the great big fish that had been caught on that very spot. A nearby fisherman was telling me all the joy and rewards of being patient. Sure enough, as if by magic, my patience paid off. I caught a huge fish. It must have measured close to six or even eight inches long; easily enough to feed the whole family. "What kind of a fish is it?" I asked proudly. "Why that's a Cape May Goodie," came the straight-faced answer.

We all dined on the magic fish that night. It didn't take too long to debunk the name of that wonderful fish nor the fact that it had a little help supplying dinner for all those mouths. However I must, with red face admit, I just recently learned the whole truth. While I had been distracted by the neighborly fisherman, my aunt had hung the fish on my line. I had not been Captain Ahab after all; I had been the great white fish!!!

Oh, well! What did I know? I was busy being hooked.

Chapter Sixty-Four

V. J. Day

When the announcement came on the radio that the war was over, I was at someone else's house with my parents, I'm not sure who's house, but I remember being under the dining room table playing. At first I was driving a submarine, and then I was hiding from a herd of adults running around and yelling. It's funny how something can be frightening and good at the same time. Everyone was yelling yet somehow I knew it was ok. Still, I thought it might be a good idea not to get stepped on. I stayed in my shelter and watched the pandemonium. Soon I was scooped up and put into a stroller with one of my sisters, probably Rita, and was wheeled through streets, just as loud and wild as the house we had just left. I guess we eventually got home, because the next thing I remember is all the kids in the neighborhood, and all of their bikes done up fine, in red-white-and-blue crepe paper and being involved in a spontaneous parade. The revelry seemed to go on for days. These were happy times. One by one, my uncles began to come home.

One by one, all the soldiers came home . . . all the soldiers who were going to come home. One by one the stars disappeared from the windows, gone were the ration books and the bond drives. Slowly the war began to fade into the past. Thus began a happy and naïve time, the "fabulous fifties." Yes, I know there were five years between the end of the war and the beginning of the fifties but, trust me, when the war ended, the fifties began. Happy days!!!

Chapter Sixty-Five

The Fifties

Happy days they were indeed, honestly, the fifties were a great time to be a teenager. Throughout history young people have always been foolish and rebellious in their attempt to cross over from childhood to adulthood. We seemed to take it a step or two further in both rebelliousness and in foolishness. Consider, if you will, the dress code of the fifties.

A "white on white," or "pink on pink," shirt with a Mr. "B" collar . . . a knitted slim Jim tie (black or pink), a super skinny suede belt to match the tie . . . a pair of black shadows or powder blues with saddle stitching and pistol pockets and with a high rise and a tight "peg, . . ." and a one-button link with tear drops. Either box-toed loafers or a pair of Flag Fliers . . . a gun metal gray "Six Button Benny" . . . and set it all off with a Flat Top, a T.C. Roll, and a D.A.

No I'm not speaking a foreign language, I'm just dressing for a Saturday night, circa nineteen-fifty something. Teenagers have always acted and dressed strangely from "Flappers to Hip Hop" but we in the fifties seemed to excel at the challenge. Truly, looking back with a little detachment, we couldn't have been funnier looking if we had tried. (And I sometimes think we *did* try.)

There I was, dressed to the nines and headed to the dance, "In line and feeling fine." This brings up the subject of music. Now I know they don't write really good meaningful songs anymore, like they did when I was young: songs with sweet tender words like "Ling Ting Tong" and "Long Tall Sally," calm and soothing melodies like the beautiful "Lama Lama Ding Dong" or "Splish Splash" (I was taking a bath). I've heard it said that the birth of Rock and Roll was the death of music. I don't think I would go quite that far . . . but, we sure scared the hell out of it. I think maybe we scared our parents as well. Between the ways we dressed, our music, and the way we talked it's almost enough to scare me. But, like, man it was, like, harmless . . . I, like to think it was, like, cool man cool. It was also groovy and a bunch of other adjectives that I'd just as soon not remember. It's fun to look at old photos, and "remember when." . . . This is fun, but a little embarrassing too. It also takes some of the sting out of my assessments of young people and makes it difficult to keep a straight face. You can't take yourself too seriously when faced with your own past in pictures . . . even if you were just a kid.

Chapter Sixty-Six

The Big Fight

I hung out with a good bunch of kids. Like me, they teetered between innocent naiveté and outright criminality. Our headquarters was a small neighborhood candy store. We were never real criminals unless nuisance was a crime; however, we did excel at being a "pain in the butt."

One hot summer night, we were sitting around, doing nothing, like most nights, listening to the jukebox and hanging out. Suddenly, there was a loud crash, we all ran to see what had happened. There was an accident where two trucks had really whacked each other. Both were out of service. I don't even remember what the one truck was but, the other one was a pie truck. Yes, a pie truck. The people that owned it came with another small truck and took everything except a rack full of pies. They were a little disheveled, but otherwise perfect. Orphaned, but perfect. The people who had been in charge of them were just barely out of sight when we ran to take advantage of, what was obviously, an open invitation. There were maybe a dozen of us and at least twice as many pies, maybe more. The only problem was they were all blueberry. How many whole blueberry pies can you eat at one sitting? While we were sitting there doing nothing but stuffing our faces in time to the music, another accident occurred. Well, it was sort of an accident. One of the girls was moving from one spot to another when she hit me in the head, not on purpose, but in the spirit of the moment, I retaliated. Now I must pause here to tell you that at that time, among other fads, girls wore white jeans. My instinctive reaction was to slap her on the butt; I had not stopped to think about the blueberry pies or their residue on my hands. There, imprinted on the seat of her britches, was a perfect blueberry hand-print. She casually remarked "#@**" and with lady-like gentility replied with a handful of blueberry pie filling. As if it were a well-rehearsed dance, everyone jumped to their feet and grabbed a hand-ful of pie with which to defend themselves.

At first whole pies were flying, then we were reduced to scrapping up handfuls of blueberry goo and making dirty, purple snowballs. People came out of their houses and out of the candy store to see what all the noise was about. Soon, by accident or design, they were involved. Warriors fought as singles or in improvised teams. The blue goo was everywhere and the fight raged on. I have no idea of the grand total of participants as some were total strangers who had just happened by and couldn't resist the temptation. A trolley car came along and stopped for the fools in the street throwing blueberries, it didn't take too long before they were involved as well. All in all it was the biggest and best pie fight ever. After hostilities had terminated, we were left there with a blue world. The whole world was dripping with blue goo—the whole world and everyone in it. We turned on the fire hydrant and, as best we could, tried to clean up the mess, naturally a small water fight ensued. Let me tell you blueberries stain, they really stain! Sometime later I told this story to my wife, she smiled and said that maybe I was stretching the truth just a bit. We later had occasion to be in the old neighborhood while returning from downtown. I took advantage of the opportunity and drove past the corner where the infamous event had taken place. There, on the wall of the old empty factory building, across the street from the now abandoned candy store, on the faded yellow paint from the sign where the business name had been, was a large blue stain . . .

. . . a stain that shouted, "Blueberry pie fight, yahoo!!!"

Chapter Sixty-Seven

The Little Green Ghost

While I'm on the trail of colorful stories, let me tell you the story of the green ghost. No, it's not a Halloween story, this ghost was a green mouse.

I was never the ideal student, but, I made up for being a slow learner with poor behavior. Let's say I was high spirited. The story begins with a math teacher—a nice person and a good teacher. One of those teachers that was able to make math interesting and easy to learn. Unfortunately, also a teacher that took sick and had to take off the rest of the year. What had started out to be a very promising year went downhill precipitously. The replacement teacher was somewhat less qualified and, in fact, spent a good deal of time doing crossword puzzles. This led to a dangerous level of boredom for the class. As if to add insult to injury, this teacher was inept and indifferent, had a nasty edge, and seemed to purposely try to belittle students . . . bad idea! Never aggravate energetic young people, especially when they outnumber you twenty to one. Oh yes! One more factor that I failed to mention; the alleged teacher also had a little problem with excessive adult beverage intake. This fact led to the germ of an idea. A small group of us took a large mouse and with some green ink dyed it a new color. Now, what do we do with our psychedelic pet? Naturally we took it to class just to think things over. While our guest was visiting, it was seen, and we knew it had been spotted. We were expecting an explosion any second; instead, a strange thing happened. The teacher took a break for a little refreshment, for nerve before investigation, but then made believe nothing had happened. By now our guest was safely back in the Hop-a-long Cassidy lunch box it called home.

Every class had a "goodie-two-shoes" who delights in telling all. This teacher had even succeeded in alienating the class nerd. With one hundred percent participation from the class and the unbelieving reaction from the teacher, we knew we were on a roll. For the remainder of the year the reaction randomly alternated between an all-knowing "Ah ha!" at nothing, and just trying to pretend that nothing had happened. No one, not the teacher or the class, ever spoke a word about the green mouse in the inkwells. Maybe it was real, then again, maybe it wasn't. Sometimes two or three times, and sometimes not at all, the little green ghost would appear. Then disappear quickly. After this, it was passed, in the blink of an eye, back to its little tin home. What started out as a one time "pay back" ended up lasting the better part of a school year. Since we weren't learning anything anyway, we found a way to keep busy. It wasn't too difficult to take advantage of that pour soul. The hard part was not rolling on the floor with laughter. We did a lot of putting our heads down and stifling. I don't think we did too much to help with the beverage problem, but we managed to cure our boredom. Kids will be kids, especially if you mistreat them.

Chapter Sixty-Eight

Getting Rid of Rags

I've told you already that Saturdays were magic, and magic they truly were. At different ages, for different reasons, but always magic. At this time the magic was "butter roll buns." The city, in those days, had lots of bakeries. They were small family businesses usually in a corner store. There were at least a half dozen within easy walking distance of our home. They each seemed to have a specialty. One would specialize in cheese cake, and another in sticky buns, and so on. There was a bakery we called the "D" Street Bakery. Their special was the butter roll bun which was a delicious cross between a cinnamon bun and Danish. Saturday mornings were a magic mixture of sweet cakes and coffee. Now, somebody had to go get this magic treat. My mother picked two "somebodies;" my sister and me.

This day, while on our quest, we met a stranger—the skinniest, dirtiest, and ugliest dog that the good Lord ever made. We made friends with this poor mutt on the way to the store and to our delight he was still hanging around on the way home. With only a little encouragement and a little help from a clothesline around his neck, he followed us home. The clothesline was a contribution from a nearby yard. They'll never miss it. Once we reached home, everybody fell in love with this dirty and disheveled dog. For better or worse, he was now a part of the family. With a great deal of energy he was bathed and brushed, and I must say that once he was cleaned up, he was still ugly. He was a little bit of every color you can think of. The color pattern was not in spots or patches, but more like God had stood back and thrown the colors at him. He looked for all the world like a "Rag Mop," which happened to be the title of a popular song at the time. It naturally became his theme song, to my constant amusement, and his name became "Rag Mop" or "Rags" for short.

Rags was very enthusiastic. The truth be known, I never figured out what it was he was so enthused over, but he sure was wired about something. Another one of his qualities was that he was dumb as a stump. If you look up dumb dog in the great encyclopedia of life, there is a picture of Rags. My father tried to train him, with unlimited patience and the use of treats. Rags said, "Oh boy treats! I like treats! I get treats for going to the bathroom. Wow." The next time he went on the kitchen floor, he came looking for my father to show him and get a treat. The poor beast was panting and jumping around proud as all get out, "Look what I did." He eventually got a little better but he never really succeeded in understanding the underlying principal. He did, however, succeed in wearing out his welcome with my Dad. He said he was tired of finding land mines "the hard way." He explained as to how it was beginning to ruin his mornings. His cure for the problem was something that was common then, but that we would never do today. Rags went for a ride to New Jersey.

The thinking back then was that if you turned him loose in the woods he would be fine as a wild dog and no one would be harmed. Now, not only was this not a good way of disposing of unwanted pets, but Rags didn't agree with it either. My Dad found a good spot deep in the woods, gave him a big bone and headed home. I don't know what he was thinking about on that long trip, but I'm sure he was greatly relieved to be rid of that pest. When at last he arrived home, guess who was waiting on the front steps? With his tail wagging and happy to see that my Dad got home safely, that dog still had his bone in his mouth. He won a reprieve, if not a pardon. But alas and alack, the experience didn't make him any smarter, and soon he was back in the doghouse, so to speak. Since losing him was out of the question another answer had to be found. As usual, my Dad came up with a new plan. It seemed that a man he knew from work lived on a farm outside of the city and was willing to take the dumb dog. The way my father described him was, "He's a very nice man, not the brightest bulb in the chandelier, but very likable." Let me tell you, that was a match made in heaven. The last I heard, Rags was the daddy of a large litter of pups. Like their dad, they were all ugly as mud and dumb as a stump, but full of enthusiasm and very loveable.

"Rag Mop Doodle ee oo daa de ah da."

Chapter Sixty-Nine

Who Killed Howdy Doody?

When I was still very young, one of my prized possessions was a Howdy Doody hand puppet. It was a dumb thing and I
was fast outgrowing it. I didn't want to, but I was.

It was one of those little crises that all children go through.
I was at that awkward age when you want to be a big kid but you
don't want to grow up. I was just old enough to know about Santa
but young enough to still believe, because I still wanted to. It's a
crying shame that children have to grow up at all but it's downright
painful for them to be caught in between—too old for baby toys
and not yet old enough to play with the big kids. That puppet was
one of the last outposts in my babyhood. I didn't often play with it
anymore, it was too babyish, but sometimes when no one else was
around . . . well . . .

One sad day I came home from school to find that someone
had killed poor Howdy. His body was made of cloth and fit on your
hand like a glove. His large, colorful head was made of rubber and
had a fittingly large mouth—all in all, a handsome and clever

companion. (I was much too big to have a doll.) Someone had indeed done in Doody. His already large mouth now ran all the way to his ear. It looked as if he had been caught squealing on the Mob, or perhaps Mr. Bluster had hired the Mafia to take over the Doodyville Circus. Whatever the case, poor Doody was dead. Something was rotten in the peanut gallery, and I was brokenhearted. I was more so, perhaps, because in a very short while I would have completely outgrown it. In its own good time it would have been relegated to the dark recesses of a closet. But that would be then and this was now, and I was not ready.

Indignant and offended I initiated a coroner's inquest. Then, with all the acumen of Sherlock Holmes and using my vast powers of deduction, I caught the culprit. Actually, I screamed at the top of my lungs, "Who ripped my puppet?" Little sister Judy ran, in fear for her life, and hid behind her mother. (Coincidentally, she also happened to be *my* mother) Our Mom had a calming way about her and she took charge of the situation. There would be no lynching, no tar and feathers; I couldn't even give her a shot in the eye. Sometimes there's just no justice. My Mom explained that it had been an accidental assassination. It had something to do with a medical experiment gone wrong. The test was to see just how wide his mouth would open. There was a long grieving process but eventually I outgrew this tragedy. Although, I still have a soft spot for Howdy Doody and an abiding fear of opening my big mouth too near to little sister Judy.

Chapter Seventy

Memories

Among my happiest memories is coming home from school. The radio was on softly, and the afternoon sun made the room warm and bright with color. My Mom was at the kitchen stove stirring "Poor Man's Cake"—a wonderful aromatic concoction somewhere between fruitcake and homemade bread. It didn't much matter what was for dinner. That night I knew what was for dessert. Dinner could have been: homestyle macaroni, baked beans and ground meat, ground meat and gravy, corned beef hash, or any one of an almost endless string of old recipes; the lady was magic. I always said someday I would open a restaurant called "The Depression Diner" and share with the world all those delightful tastes and treats from bygone days. Those were days of making lots from little and excellent from adequate. Then again, maybe the world is not quite ready for that. Maybe I'll start with just a cookbook. Maybe I'll just continue to think and remember the way it was when I would sit and relax with a warm slice of Poor Man's Cake with butter on it, a fresh hot cup of coffee, a soft radio in the background, and a whole room full of memories. I can only wish you as much joy in whatever warms your heart when you sit by yourself and remember. Even if we were just a couple of kids . . . we knew what was important.

Chapter Seventy-One

You may have noticed this has not been a chronology like the history you hated in school. It has been more a series of vignettes, like flashes of memories that jump forward and backward in time. It is very much like playing "remember when" while sitting around the table with family and friends. Enjoy a glass of wine, a cup of coffee, and endless stories since each story reminds you of another. There is a feeling you can get no place else. Pull up a chair, the laughs are just starting, the love has always been. Welcome to our family table, share a tale or two from your "remember when."

As for me, I have three children who live in Hawaii, one who lives in New York and thank God, one who lives close by. I very much love and miss them all and appreciate to no end the time we have together. It's unbelievable how much it brightens a day to hear from them and from their children. As for the poor soul that lives closest to me, I love and appreciate, and often take shameless advantage of him. Fortunately, he is very generous with his time, talent and patience.

Eventually I got old. I never did grow up and I don't plan to. I'm still the little kid from Bologna Row and proud of it. Then again, what do I know, I'm still just a kid.

I hope you enjoyed my childhood. I tried hard to remember only the best for you. If it pleased you, please thank all the wonderful people that made it such a joy for me.

Heaven knows, I sure do. . . .

God bless,

T.J.G.

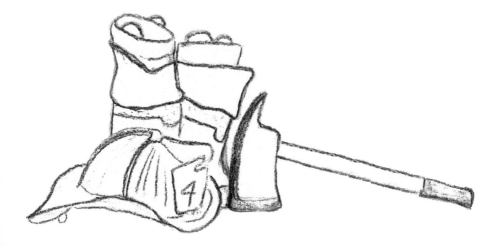

Where is That Kid?

Where? Oh where is that little guy,
That kid from Bologna Row?
What became of his twinkling eye,
And the smile I used to know?

It doesn't seem all that long ago,
That he was playing there—
In his dungarees and an old polo,
And his head full of curly hair.

It hardly seems to be a blink,
Or a turn of the old clock's dial.
It's hard for me to even think,
That it has been such a long, long while.

The years have fled, I don't know how,
But gone are those precious hours.
And we must live in the here and now,
Until it flees like those summer showers.

He doesn't look like he once did,
Nor dress like in times gone by,
But he is still that little kid,
Though a little sad of eye.

For now that kid is turning gray,
And he plays a different game,
But still remembers that long lost day,
And inside he feels the same. . . .

T.J.G.